myriad intimacies

lata mani ▼

myriad intimacies

DUKE UNIVERSITY PRESS Durham and London 2022

Designed by Aimee C. Harrison
Typeset in Garamond Premier Pro by Westchester Publishing Services

Library of Congress Cataloging-in-Publication Data
Names: Mani, Lata, [date] author.
Title: Myriad intimacies / Lata Mani.
Description: Durham : Duke University Press, 2022. | Includes
bibliographical references.
Identifiers: LCCN 2021035743 (print)
LCCN 2021035744 (ebook)
ISBN 9781478015659 (hardcover)
ISBN 9781478018278 (paperback)
ISBN 9781478022886 (ebook)
Subjects: LCSH: Religion and culture. | Tantrism. | Ontology. | Social
justice. | Criticism—Political aspects. | BISAC: RELIGION / Spirituality
Classification: LCC BL65.C8 M3525 2022 (print) | LCC BL65.C8 (ebook) |
DDC 306.6—dc23/eng/20211021
LC record available at https://lccn.loc.gov/2021035743
LC ebook record available at https://lccn.loc.gov/2021035744

Cover art: Untitled, anonymous, near Udaipur, 1999. From *Tantra
Song: Tantric Painting from Rajasthan*, edited by Franck André Jamme
(Catskill, NY: Siglio Press), 2011.

for
all that I have been taught
all that I have yet to learn

contents

videos with nicolás grandi

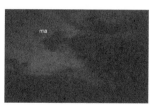

Videos can be accessed by scanning the QR Code below.

https://doi.org/10.6084/m9.figshare.c.5707808

acknowledgments

WE CAN BE ONLY partially aware of all that has activated and sustained our work. For, in addition to what we know to have prompted reflection—current events, ongoing debates, reigning assumptions—there is the enigma of how the moon and stars, the tamarind and redwood trees, the chance remark and musical phrase impelled us to bring something flickering at the edge of consciousness to the center of our awareness. To this mystery I first bow.

As an endeavor not grounded in a single discipline or focused on one demarcatable question, *Myriad Intimacies* is located within multiple, overlapping conversations. Such a text is bound to exclude references to works that also belong within its citational universe. To the inevitability of this fact I add the following circumstance: I suffered a brain injury in 1993, which has made reading long articles and books virtually impossible. It has led me to work intuitively, from memory, observation, and contemplation rather than research and a close reading of texts, as I had previously done. Although I have learned from listening to subsequent scholarship via talks uploaded on the web, this process enables me to cite the broad contours of an argument, not its details. I invite readers to inscribe in the text's margins additional references that would extend and enrich the questions posed here. ♥

I began the work collected in *Myriad Intimacies* in Bangalore, India, and completed it in Oakland, California. It interweaves my writing with my video collaborations with Nicolás Grandi. Nicolás and I met in Bangalore when he was teaching film and video at the Srishti School of Art, Design and Technology. We started working together just as he was preparing to return to Buenos Aires. Our transoceanic partnership would have been impossible were it not for the synergy of our relationship and the possibilities unleashed by the internet. Working with Nicolás has nudged me to move beyond print in exploring the potential of transmedia experiments to pluralize perception. I thank all who have collaborated with us in our projects.

Early iterations of some of the material in *Myriad Intimacies* were presented at Goldsmiths, University of London, University of California, Los Angeles, University of California, Berkeley, University of British Columbia, Vancouver, University of Amsterdam, and Princeton University. I am grateful to my interlocutors at these events, for their comments served to hone my thinking.

Deepa Dhanraj listened at all hours, as did Sowmya Ramanathan who in addition graciously undertook impromptu requests for bibliographic assistance. My sisters, Meera and Sunita Mani, provided a home away from home. Avtar Brah, Indira Chowdhury, Vivek Dhareshwar, Rosa Linda Fregoso, Akhil Gupta, and Purnima Mankekar offered the sustenance of conversation and friendship. Bach, Handel, jazz, *slokas*, *dhrupad*, and Sufi music were the soundtrack of my days, with rock periodically stepping in to ground my energy. The unseen was a constant, sheltering presence.

Last but not least I thank Ken Wissoker for soliciting this manuscript and gently persuading me that it had a home at Duke University Press.

▼

The following were initially guest posts on the online blog *Kafila*: "A Glorious Thing Made Up of Stardust: What Pat Parker & Rohith Vemula Ask Us to Consider," February 19, 2016; "Am I Doing Enough? Crisis, Activism & the Search for Meaning," March 14, 2016; "Sticks and Stones May Break my Bones . . . but Words? On the Rhetoric of Social Justice Activism," April 1, 2016; "Objects in the Mirror are Closer Than You Think: Beyond the Rhetoric of Otherness," November 12, 2017. "A Malleable Border Teeming with Life," was first posted June 2, 2020, on the website *Solidarity and Care During the Covid-19 Pandemic*. "We Inter Are: Identity Politics & #MeToo" was published in *Feminist Review* 122, no. 1 (2019): 198–204. All are reprinted here with permission.

In your hand this book
Object unto itself
Essays Poems Process Notes
Analytical   Contemplative

This book in your hands
An effect of your reading
Juxtapositions   sequences
Encountered in print-duration
Interleaving these
Links to video experimentations
Sensorial landscapes
Temporal explorations

It is hoped that you will accept these
As linked invitations
To play & engage with
Proposed interpretations

introduction ▼ integral entanglements, formal experiments

Myriad Intimacies is conceived as an offering. It comprises prose, poetry, and audiovisual explorations of the interrelatedness of lives, life forms, concepts, and frameworks. *Myriad Intimacies* is not an *intervention*, a term that implies pointed interjection in a stable, preconstituted domain of inquiry. Even when addressing issues with a rich discursive history—identity, otherness, political rhetoric—the approach is exploratory in order to enact ideas in the mode of address, to offer a cumulative experience of them by interleaving genres and forms. The word *offering* has a distinctly spiritual connotation. This association makes it especially appropriate because this collection moves freely, unapologetically, between registers that would be distinguished as "sacred" or "secular" and not customarily found within the covers of a single work. The method I adopt here was developed well before COVID-19, in whose shadow I completed the manuscript. But it seems especially apposite when the impact of the virus on every aspect of life means that the term *existential* was for once being collectively experienced in both its material and its philosophical sense.

We live and work in contexts in which a narrowly instrumental notion of knowledge is dominant. We are primarily addressed as *homo economicus*, and within that categorization as consumers first and foremost. What has manifested is a logic of proliferation within an increasingly narrow conception of possibilities and, relatedly, ever greater conformism masquerading as affirmation of infinite potential and creativity. Even debates on the plurality and fluidity of identity have at times become entangled with these dynamics, multiplying categories rather than challenging their premises. Critique has become a commodity to be consumed. We are rarely addressed as philosophical beings engaged by broader questions of what it means to be human, though climate change and the intense precarity of neoliberalism have brought these issues into relief, a process further accelerated by the COVID-19 pandemic and the uprisings against racial injustice in the wake of George Floyd's murder by Minneapolis police.

The idea of the socio-natural world as an autonomous entity—one separable from the observer and awaiting cognitive capture by an objective researcher—has continued to prevail despite the cumulative and fatal challenges to it from multiple, overlapping directions: critical studies of science; critique of Enlightenment philosophy; feminism; new materialisms; quantum physics; indigenous epistemologies; postcolonial, race, and cultural studies. Several generations of scholars have contributed to these complex developments, including Jacqui M. Alexander (2006), Gloria Anzaldúa (1987), Arjun Appadurai (1996), Karan Barad (2007), Rosi Braidotti (2013, 2019), Dipesh Chakravarty (2000, 2018), Marisol de la Cadena (2015), Arturo Escobar (2018), Stuart Hall (1996, 2019a, b), or Donna Haraway (1991, 2003, 2008, 2016), Bruno Latour (2017, 2018), Trinh T. Minh-ha (1989), Cherríe Moraga (2011; see also Moraga's 1981 publication with Anzaldúa), Elizabeth Povinelli (2016), Edward Said (1979), Isabelle Stengers (2010, 2011), and Anna Tsing (2015).

The compelling and forceful nature of the combined critique should have remade knowledge and put paid to the notion of objective universal truth. But the critique has been contained within certain disciplines, segregated into particular branches within disciplines, or accommodated by a softening of the borders of what is deemed permissible as an argument or the form in which it can be presented. For the most part, the dominant norms of power and authority have remained intact.

Genuine inquiry involves inhabiting a space between cognitive abeyance and cognitive freefall. Until, gradually, cumulatively, nonlinearly, and retroactively, one marshals conceptual and empirical resources to elucidate the intuitions that have prompted one's investigation. It is an unpredictable process that can require one to recast initial questions or even abandon them in order to travel in an altogether different direction. And yet scholarly protocol often obscures the very process by which knowledge comes into being. Or else it only partially discloses it. The authoritativeness of a finished work can occlude the destabilizing uncertainty of inquiry. It can seem as though the argument was evident to the author and merely needed to be put down in order that it may be shared with others. Is it any wonder that an overly stable conception of knowledge is continually fortified?

▼

The work gathered in *Myriad Intimacies* is grounded in the following propositions:

- We are sensuous beings inhabiting "infinity," a continually evolving, multiply and mutually constituted field of interrelations. Our senses compose our material experience. We apprehend the world through them.
- We have at our disposal language that by its nature constrains our imagination even as it unleashes it.
- Any analytic effort can only trace some aspects of the manifold cause-and-effect interrelations that bear on the issue at hand. The omnipotent researcher with mastery over her object of study makes way for the modest explorer who is conscious of the rich specificity and partiality of her understanding.
- We are situated, sentient beings. The stories we tell locate us (Haraway 1988; Mohanty 1987).
- The idea of knowledge as capture is an untenable fiction and would do well to cede ground to <u>knowing as a practice of attunement.</u>

It might seem odd to name infinity as an interpretive horizon, because as humanists our work primarily addresses the social world. I invoke infinity as a way to alert us to the danger that the focus we are required to develop might lead us to forget that from a planetary perspective, from the purview of the cosmos, our work is irreducibly local. For we are thinking with/of/about particular specificities and their evolving, multiply constituted, embedded mutualities.

At the heart of my efforts to counter the inertia of present norms has been a rethinking of time, form, and structure. Time, form, and structure are closely interrelated, and what it means to experiment with them in writing and in video varies given the specificities of each medium. It has meant rethinking "argument" as the dispersed cumulative effect of composing and arranging pieces so as to enable a polyphonic experience of key ideas. The essays are short by design so that the invitation to consider core propositions can be made gradually, evocatively, and severally via the forms that comprise a given work. But whereas my previous books, *SacredSecular: Contemplative Cultural Critique* (2009) and *The Integral Nature of Things: Critical Reflections on the Present* (2013), experimented with observational writing, poetry, and contemplative and analytical prose, *Myriad Intimacies* goes further by interweaving multigenre writing with videopoems and video-contemplations. Moving between genres and mediums organically disrupts normative expectations. The reader/viewer is continually repositioned in relation to the work and is required to adjust to shifts in language, focus, mood, and depth of perception. The form and structure make evident the processual nature of interpretation, and the linguistic and visual play it enables serves to unsettle representation as a forensic craft devoid of mystery.

Myriad Intimacies can be described as a narrative whole composed of fragments. *Fragment*, defined as remnant, portion, incomplete part, derives from the Latin *frangere*, to break.

Also from *frangere*:

> *fraction* (a proportion of a whole number)
> *fracture* (crack, break)
> *fractious* (quarrelsome)

It might seem that portion, part, incompleteness, brokenness, and ill-temperedness are indelibly linked.

Frangere, however, is also the root for *fractal*. This fact brings into view a different, more expansive, dimension. A fractal is a geometric figure or natural phenomenon in which a repeated pattern can be observed at each scale of magnification. Such repetitions may be identical or to varying degrees self-similar. Mathematician Benoît Mandelbrot (1982) coined the term to redress the shortcomings of classical geometry in describing the complexity of a whole range of natural phenomena, among them snow-flakes, trees, plants, river networks, and cardiovascular systems. Fractal patterns have since been observed in, and inspired the making of, art, image, sound, music.

Interpretation is an exercise in composition and framing. As I already noted, it involves noticing some things from among a near-infinite range of possibilities and striving to understand the relationships between them. One can neither "see everything" nor make sense of all of the interrelationships between what one beholds. By its nature interpretation is a continual, always partial, process of building from fragments and developing principles for moving between and among them. Fractals affirm the insights of contemplative teaching regarding the inseparability of part and whole. In the seed, the tree. Out of one, many. To contemplate is to observe closely, to understand through analysis and reflection, a process that is at once both outward and inward, as the world is first encountered within. Observation, analysis, reflection: forms of magnification that oscillate between proximity and distance, focusing in and then widening the frame.

Expansion, contraction: inhalation, exhalation. A "natural" rhythm but also one crucial to inquiry as sensuous dispassion: a fullness of presence that can activate a curiosity and hold habitual perception in check. Honoring this dynamic implies and requires a certain pacing in writing, structure, composition, editing. S-t-r-e-t-c-h-i-n-g time and e l o n g a t i n g attention to allow for the possibility of seeing anew, moving through cognitive and physical discomfort toward terra (as yet) incognita.

Although considered uniquely contemporary, transmedia and multigenre explorations are arguably current iterations of an ancient pedagogy rooted in the premise that beings learn in accordance with their nature. It is for this reason that in Hindu-Buddhist traditions, the mandala or yantra (a geometric representation of the journey of the practitioner) has many doorways. It is assumed that each individual will enter through the portal most suited to them and navigate the labyrinth of inquiry in their own way. Thus, also in indigenous and other storytelling traditions one finds a plethora of stories, a proliferation of metaphors, accordion-like narrative structures that facilitate digression, interpolations, narrative recursivity, and so on. These forms are capacious enough for a spiritual or philosophical investigation, able to hold paradox, contradiction, and multiple valences.

A kaleidoscopic approach in which core ideas are explored in various distinct and overlapping ways is one means of responding to the crisis of perception we confront today. For it is not a paucity of information that accounts for an absence of fellow feeling but rather the absence of fellow feeling that estranges us from the facts and their implications. Fake news or information silos are merely a secondary manifestation of the severing of the truth of our interrelatedness. This divisiveness and sense of separation are not merely problems of genre. Yet genre experiments are one means of embedding generosity and extending trust to the reader/viewer. To this end, *Myriad Intimacies* is intentionally crafted so relative autonomy exists in the relationships between elements, between chapters or sections, within chapters, and between kinds of writing and visual representation. Even though the book is meant to be grasped in its totality, each aspect or segment is not conceived as subsidiary and fully subsumable within it. Rather, each element exists in a dual sense: as itself and in particular relation to the work as a whole. This orientation enables me to be cognitively honest about sense-making as provisional synthesis, to trust readers/viewers to make their own way through the material, to navigate its surprises, its incompleteness, as they choose. In moving between different densities of expression, they can experience nonfiction as an encounter with multiple temporalities.

The analytical terms that frame this text are probably familiar to most readers—all, that is, barring one: *tantra*. As a term, *tantra* is found within the assemblage of ideas and practices designated today as "Hinduism" and in Buddhism. But as a philosophical orientation it is not unique to these traditions, and indeed, although present in them, not as widely practiced as one might wish. A brief introduction may thus be appropriate.

Tantra conceives the universe as sentient and all life forms within it as equal. This egalitarian assessment extends to all life activity as well. Tantra honors embodiment as sacred, the senses as a form of intelligence, and each living entity as existing in two interlinked triadic relationships: self-other-connectivity; self-other-divinity. To honor those who may be skeptical of the idea of spirit or divinity, when appropriate I substitute *laws of nature* for *laws of creation*. This substitution is not a concession, because within a tantric perspective the rest of nature unresistingly manifests the laws of creation. It is we humans who, endowed with free will, can choose whether or not to live by them. To coerce us to do so would be to violate the gift given to us.

I should clarify that the understanding of tantra on which I draw here is gleaned from a long-term practice of meditation and not from a scholarly study of Hindu-Buddhist tantric texts. In so doing I tread a path that reflects South Asian spiritual pedagogy, which is as rooted in insights derived from practice as in those arising from textual study, and in which texts themselves are understood to be post hoc compilations of wisdom yielded by practice. I will say more about tantra in the pages that follow but only to an extent relevant to a text seeking to braid secular and spiritual inquiry and transcode between ways of knowing. Readers who are curious about the particular iteration of the philosophy that informs this work may turn to *The Tantra Chronicles*, a compendium of received teachings (Frankenberg and Mani, 2013). I hope this preliminary sketch has indicated why tantra might be relevant to a humanity fatally divided against itself and to a world battered by a disdain for nature. A world that, even through its bruising, spins steadily on its axis, inviting us to see it anew and in so doing renew ourselves and all that makes life possible.

one ▼ the COVID-19 pandemic

A TANTRIC INVITATION TO HUMANITY

SNAPSHOT: December 2020. It is close to a year since COVID-19 brought humanity to its knees. Across the world economic activity has seized or severely contracted as lockdowns were imposed, lifted, and reimposed in response to the rise and fall of infections. Despite forewarning from public health experts about the potential for such a cataclysmic global event, few governments were prepared for it. Decades of short-term thinking and austerity economics driven by corporate greed and profiteering left nations poorly equipped to tackle the crisis. Governments have largely responded with old playbooks that are insufficient for the scale of the problem at hand. Some continue to insist against all evidence that COVID-19 is not a crisis. In the year 2020, whose numerals signify perfect vision, virtually nothing is clear except how we got here. And for this wisdom we may thank all those communities, activists, researchers, analysts, artists, and others who have been patiently sounding the alarm about humanity's dance with destruction and extinction.

As the months have gone by, it has become increasingly evident that this problem is not one that can be solved at the level of the problem. It is not only a question of a vaccine effective against inevitable variants and the gargantuan task of its equitable global distribution. Or one of ensuring better wages. Or bolstering public health. Or reviving domestic production given the perils of an overreliance on global supply chains. Or restoring regulatory oversight, labor rights, respect for the rule of law. Or voting out lethally incompetent governments. All these actions would certainly make a significant difference. But there is a gnawing, growing sense that even as these solutions seem difficult—even impossible—to achieve given prevailing economic and political structures, more to the point they may be patently insufficient, like taking a watering can to a forest fire. This sense is why listening to the news or keeping abreast of analysis fails to soothe or bring narrative order to the chaos and uncertainty that has defined this period. COVID-19 is not, as many rightly suspect, just a contagious virus. It is above all a crisis of perception, posing fundamental questions about the "how," "what," and "why" of life. An invitation to emerge and see.

▼

Tantra begins with the premise that the universe is sentient. Everything that exists in the universe is alive and in a complex, mutually constitutive relationship with everything else. To put it more simply, everything exists relationally, nothing in isolation. We may not understand the interrelations between all that exists, but that does not call into question the fact of relationality. Another premise of tantra is that all matter has integrity and that embodiment is sacred. Building on these presuppositions, tantra posits the senses as a pathway to knowledge.

The current pandemic is generally considered a state of exception. But a state of exception is frequently a moment that unequivocally clarifies what has always been true, though it may not have been properly acknowledged and may even have been denied. Regardless of how differently we are affected by COVID-19—and very material differences exist depending on class, race, gender, caste, sexuality, age, geographical location, and so on—the virus compels us to recognize our interrelatedness: not just with other humans but with the rest of nature. We are deeply interconnected with all that exists—a fact we have refused to acknowledge fully. It turns out that our lives depend on such recognition.

During the postindustrial period, humans have arrogated the right to willfully destroy nature and remake matter as we see fit. Matter has been considered inert and without intrinsic value until human labor makes it productive for circulation within the economy. We have celebrated human ingenuity to remake the world as a playground for humanity—not all of humanity, for sure, but for our species alone. In the process we have exploited or ignored the needs and habitats of the millions of life forms with which we share the planet: animal, vegetable, mineral, microbial. Our actions have profoundly affected them all. And their destinies, as some of us are beginning to realize, with horror, are intimately tied to our own.

From a tantric perspective this is a predictable consequence of the suppositions that have guided postindustrial thinking. The interlinked, and compounding, crises we confront today of global warming, environmental degradation, desertification, pollution, rise in sea levels, and so on affirm tantric insight. The planet is a mutually re-creating, mutually sustaining nonhierarchical form of polyexistence. Diversity is its nature, relationality its grammar. Every life is deeply implicated in, imbricated with, every other life. What is true of the planet is equally true of human existence, though the terrible introduction of forms of hierarchical stratification—gender, class, race, sexuality, caste, among others—has negated the truth of human equality and interdependence.

The current crisis has brought us to the edge of a form of existence we have become accustomed to imagining as the norm. And although governments and citizenry alike continue to clamor for a return to prepandemic life, to those who are alert to the catastrophic logic of extraction at the heart of our current relationship to the rest of nature and to humans discriminated by the social order, such a return is neither feasible nor desirable. Not everyone is inclined to heed these warnings or consider bold proposals for remaking the future. Some impatiently await resumption of the status quo and give no thought to redressal or rethinking. Others are confident that temporarily enhancing investment in economic and social programs will provide the necessary safety net until we move past COVID-19. Still others doubt the very reality of the virus even as deaths mount and many who recover confront serious long-term consequences. The pandemic has devolved into a struggle over facts, how they are to be understood and what they imply about the material preconditions of our lives, and their interrelatedness.

Tantra can be an invaluable resource in meeting this moment. Tantra is a name for the triadic nature of Creation. Self-other-connectivity. Self-other-divinity. There is no self that is not connected to that which may be named not-self or other. And there is no self and no other that is not connected to spirit or divinity. Those uncomfortable with the idea of divinity can instead draw on the principles of nature in exploring tantra as framework. Biologists, geologists, botanists, ecologists all recognize that complex organisms and systems exist in relation to each other, often because of each another. And they shape each other in myriad, complex ways. Cooperation, collaboration, coexistence, mutuality: life unfolds in accordance with these principles. We have acted as though this were not true. The novel coronavirus emerged in context of human encroachment on animal habitat and biodiversity. A virus usually found in bats has spilled over into humans. The symbiosis of interdependence in turn means that the action of the virus determines whether we exist. By the same token, individual decisions to accept or resist public health guidelines are necessarily transpersonal in their impact, affecting everyone with whom we are proximate, anyone we meet, pass, touch, talk to, or brush against. The dispersion patterns of COVID-19 have dramatically revealed the ideal of the autonomous individual to be a miasma. The denial, or else the partial and inconsistent acknowledgment, of relationality—the precondition of our very existence—returns as resistance to public health efforts to mitigate spread of the virus on the grounds of liberties infringed and freedoms denied.

Thus COVID-19 seems to have brought "life itself" to a standstill—as though "life" were dependent on our activities, on our mobility; on our fulfillment of our aspirations; on our capacity to make plans and carry them out without hindrance. Granted, this description holds true for the privileged among humans. But it is surely the privileged who are most taken aback by the current turn of events. Those more chronically affected by unemployment, hunger, and lack of health care cannot be as bewildered at being unable to meet their needs or to not having their wants fulfilled as expected. For they have never had the privilege of presuming the predictability of either opportunity or outcome.

What would it mean to turn to tantra, in setting aside the delusory basis on which we have lived? It would mean falling in love with matter for its own sake, not simply as raw material for the production of value. It would mean opening ourselves cognitively, sensorially, to discovering the "isness" of everything that exists, its specific vibration, vibrancy, and form of aliveness. It would mean opening ourselves to discovering the isness of our own existence. It would mean honoring process. It would mean embracing the body. It would mean asking, among other questions, How have the facts of my densely interconnected existence remained opaque to me? How might I live if I accepted interdependence as a fact of life? What does it mean to be respons*ible*? How might I cultivate my response *abilities*? (Barad 2007; Despret 2016; Haraway 2008, 2016; Mani [2001] 2013).

The virus is not an enemy. It is the fruit of our insistent journeying into the wild whether in the laboratory or beyond without care for the consequences of our actions. A return visit from kin. It has not sought permission in requiring us to play host, and in this, too, we and it are more alike than not. During the first year of the pandemic, without the aid of a vaccine, humanity found itself in a challenging battle with an unpredictable visitor. Worldwide, more than 1.75 million people died under heartbreaking circumstances. Although they did not die so that we might live, if we stop to heed the deeper questions posed by the pandemic then maybe—just maybe—their deaths will not have been in vain.

two ▼ *the nocturnes*
with nicolás grandi

HD, 2013, 5:01/5:35 MINUTES

The
challenge of
videopoetry
an integrated encounter
of image and text

"Nocturne I," Nicolás Grandi and Lata Mani, 2013.

https://doi.org/10.6084/m9.figshare.17018615

Sound was the starting point. *Nocturne I* grew out of the symphony of urban grasslands: crickets, frogs, the occasional hoot of an owl, the whistle of a security guard, dry leaves scrunched underfoot, speech scattered by the whooshing wind. *Nocturne II* was an unexpected gift. A rare supermoon in an unusually clear Bangalore sky: an opportunity to contemplate the city's built environment.

Béla Bartók's "Musique Nocturnes" from *Out of Doors*, with its movements—its silences, the choir of creatures, near and distant sounds, the human element—opened the door to a possible structure. The soundtrack of music, nature, the human voice was composed as layers that echo, extend, interrupt, morph into each other, into silence, into digital frequencies.

When the visual assembly was almost complete, I wrote a single line of text. The words arrived as an epiphany that distilled (evocatively in *Nocturne I* and as a declaration in *Nocturne II*) the thinking that had guided the image- and sound-making process. In *Nocturne I* the text extends the visual play of shadow and light, mystery and illumination. Words appear gradually and form a sentence toward the end. By contrast, in *Nocturne II* the text announces itself in full at the start, and fragments of words flash like neon lights thereafter: *im*, *ple*, *ma*, *nence*.

The challenge of seeing in the dark contrasts with the relative ease of hearing minute noises, even their direction. A telephoto lens "carves" the darkness of the night to reveal what the human eye cannot easily see. Palm branches dissolve to reveal vertical windows lit in the far distance. A tiny dot expands into a large orange ball. Interpretation as the art of playing with the perceptual-conceptual depth of field (Mani 2015).

A recursive process: return, re-turn, place, re-place, look, listen, edit, pause, repeat, re-start. At a certain point, the form coheres enough to convey the sensory experience intended, suggesting something of an arrival.

NOCTURNE II

"Nocturne II," Nicolás Grandi and Lata Mani, 2013.

https://doi.org/10.6084/m9.figshare.17018609

three ▼ speaking to the sacred

HOW DOES ONE SPEAK TO, or of, the implicate order of the universe? To what is true but not recognized as such, at least, not by everyone? The cosmos is intrinsically worthy of reverence: Its materiality or "thingness," and that of everything within it. Its perceptible beauty. The mystery of those aspects beyond our visual or cognitive grasp. All these inspire something spacious in our consciousness. Sensations. Intuitions. The suspicion that there is a vastness of which we are a part but from which we often feel apart.

Yet language can serve to estrange us further. The very act of rendering something into existence requires stepping out and taking apart. Naming is a double-edged operation: Something is x because it is not y, or else not quite y but rather xy or yx or maybe even z, appearing as other than itself. It is via difference—through making distinctions—that we make meaning. Language stabilizes the complex and continuous dance of energy and molecules into nameable forms. Our conceptual categories and linguistic conventions attempt to tame the near-infinite pluralities in which we exist.

▼

The word *sacred* is a past participle of *sacren*, to consecrate or set apart, which in turn derives from French *sacrer* and Latin *sacer*. But this definition would imply that something must be done to matter for it to *be-*

come sacred. That the sacred is an extrinsic, not an intrinsic, attribute. Yet revered teachers (Jesus, Buddha) and celebrated teachings (Upanishadic, shamanic) propose the very opposite. They speak of *revelation, discovery, experience*. These terms imply the discovery of something that already exists. Students are urged to contemplate and discover first principles for themselves. Prayer, meditation, ceremonies, rituals, and so on are crucibles for a gradual realization and confirmation of the truth and integrity of teachings. Practice transmutes mere knowledge into active knowing. Teaching revealed in/as experience. An aide-mémoire and a pathway to re-membering.

How then are we to understand the etymology of *sacred*, noted above, in which it is deemed a consequence of human veneration and making? This idea, I argue, is a trace effect of institutional religion's arrogation of the right to determine what counts as sacred, and alongside that, the particular strand within European Enlightenment that triumphed over others and that deemed nature to be inert and human agency to be an activating force, breathing life into dead matter.

The world as intrinsically worthy of respect and reverence. To greet the world from this premise is to language the sacred from within, to draw on the methods and practices of a given tradition in order to access the interiority of consciousness and cosmos without denying each their specificity. It is not easy. Except at the hands of the most adept poet or philosopher, it can lead to linguistic mayhem. To stuttering. Muttering. Stammering. Yammering. Exhortation. Exclamation. Molten clarity. Inchoate breakdown. Prostration. Frustration. Imitation. Repetition. It can, in short, beggar language. Language trips on itself as the internal pressure builds to find expression for emergent, incipient understandings and the seeker fears imploding.

To allow the world to reveal itself is not simply to recognize, as in acknowledge, what has always been true but to re-*cognize* it, understand it anew. The process is deeply destabilizing. The astonishment and fright it can engender have produced their own term: *horripilation*. Even without recourse to a dictionary, one *feels* its meaning—hair standing erect from fear—in the effect on one's nerves of the very sound of it.

A grammar lesson. Conjugating the verb *to be*:

> I am
> You are
> He is
> She is
> We are
> You are
> They are

I/you/he/she/we/you/they, am/are/is: subject and verb placed contiguously, beside each other, in order to make meaning.

But the grammar of existence is relational. Subject and object are always already co-implicated, and every subject is always already plural. The Latin root of *conjugate—conjugare*, literally "yoked together"—captures this truth well. Zen Master Thich Nhat Hahn (1999) puts it thus: "we inter are." The prefix *inter*, common in English words deriving from Latin, means between, betwixt, among, in the midst of, mutually, reciprocal, together, during. It appositely condenses the spatial, the temporal, and the relational. We are always together, within, between, during, and among, though we may not subjectively experience the world in this way. How might our perception and experience of the world be different if we had learned to conjugate the verb *to be* as follows:

> I inter am
> You inter are
> He inter is
> She inter is
> We inter are
> You inter are
> They inter are

Grammar encodes the rules of language; language, our perceptual lens. If grammar were to reflect things as they actually are—emerging from and existing in complex, evolving dynamics of interrelatedness—false assumptions of separateness, erroneous attributions of absolute or graded difference within human-invented hierarchies, would have to be set aside as delusory.

Grammatical conventions, at least in English, contribute to obscuring the dynamics that shape how we have come to misperceive the world as we have. This process recalls the other meaning of *grammar*: magic, incantation, spells. Are our grammatical rules casting a spell on truth, rendering reality other than itself? Would the negation of nature or other beings be possible if existence were understood as a form of webbing? That "we inter are" and have always been so? No "you" without "me," no "you" who is not also "me"; yet "you," "me," not interchangeable but exquisitely distinct, like leaves on a tree, no two of which are identical. This is the implicate order of the universe. To honor it is to speak adequately to the sacred.

four ▾ the algorithm of love

Like the perfume of dense silence
the scent of jasmine enters my nostrils
and destroys all my careful calculations
Who can understand the algorithm of love
Certainly not I

five ▾ *de sidere 7*
with nicolás grandi

HD, 2014, 38:09 MINUTES

▾

In the beginning was desire

Creation
was
its
out
breath

Beware the erogenous
An error taxonomical
The division into the sexual
And the merely anatomical
As though pleasure was a calculable response
to a stimulus

And all the rest was fetish
Perversely predictable

—De Sidere 7

chapter five

"De Sidere 7," Nicolás Grandi and Lata Mani, 2014.

https://doi.org/10.6084/m9.figshare.17018600

I can't help but dream about a kind of criticism that would . . . bring . . . an idea to life; it would light fires, watch the grass grow, listen to the wind, and catch the sea foam in the breeze and scatter it. It would multiply not judgments but signs of existence; it would summon them, drag them from their sleep. Perhaps it would invent them sometimes—all the better. All the better.

        —Michel Foucault, "The Masked Philosopher"

What might it mean to refresh the image in an image-saturated world? How might one enliven the word in a high-voltage soundscape that seems inhospitable to subtlety and silence and that deadens the senses in the very process of heightening them? How can image, text, and sound cohere to open out perception, allowing us to take note of all that continues to pulse within and around us?

Foucault's longing for a new form of critique may equally be read as a call for a new kind of aesthetic practice. Indeed, he dissolves the distinction between the two domains in positing critique *as* an aesthetic practice. But that is not all. For Foucault, critique is an *embodied aesthetic practice*: "watch the grass grow, listen to the wind, and catch the sea foam in the breeze and scatter it" (1997, 323). In a further elaboration of this conception he proposes that critique multiply signs of existence, even inventing them as necessary. "All the better," he says approvingly, and repeats the phrase almost wistfully. In conceiving of critique/aesthetic practice as a simultaneous process of witnessing, inventing, and excavating, Foucault offers us an expansive notion in which thought itself emerges as a sensuous faculty.

Foucault calls on us to reimagine critique in ways that exceed the more familiar theater of encounter: confrontations structured by the dialectic of subjugation and resistance. Not because this mode of engaging power is no longer relevant, but because a great deal falls outside of this dialectic, including much that is crucial to offering a different imagination of the coexistence of species, of forms of life that can replenish. Critique must concern itself with the very texture of experience, make sensorially palpable the abstractions that shape the ruling paradigm and all that continually exceeds it.

▼

De Sidere 7 grew out of intersecting preoccupations. I had been arguing that despite being integral to sentience and beingness, desire and its close kin sensuality are understood within contemporary culture in limited and limiting ways. They had been narrowed, sequestered, instrumentalized. Desire is most proximately associated with subjectivity and sexuality; the self-determining subject is one able to actualize desire, and sexual self-determination has become a critical marker of personal freedom (Mani 2013, 2014). And in a related development that had equally to do with the instrumentalization of life in postindustrial culture and society, sensuality has been virtually conflated with the sexual. Meanwhile, Nicolás Grandi had been exploring how to think with and through specific elements of the audiovisual craft—frame, light, color, time, space, actors, subjects, props, montage cuts, sound synchresis—in order to rethink the erotics of the gaze. He was concerned with how to access and represent experience understood as a range of interdependent and plural sensations and perceptions. We both shared an interest in what a sentience-affirming aesthetic might imply.

We invited five performers to craft one or more pieces around the question, What does desire mean to you? The group included two actors, one poet-storyteller, one performance artist, and one contemporary dancer. We met twice with each to discuss their response. Our intent was to help shape their proposals without altering their core vision. Some imagined their contribution as open-ended exercises, whereas others provided more or less finished pieces. We had no prior notion of how the individual pieces would relate to each other or of the broader narrative that we would build with them. We did, however, have certain orienting principles that we extended from our previous individual work and, to a degree, from our collaborative work on the Nocturne videopoems.

The observational stance and the artistic study provided starting points. We wanted to allow the inherent logic of each performance or exercise to reveal itself. Attention to detail was crucial to such an orientation, and as with any artistic study, it was important in evolving our own understanding. We directed the performances in public places without staging them, barring one exception for which several men were recruited to form an impromptu audience (you can tell from their self-conscious demeanor that their participation was unplanned). The observational stance and artistic study also implied a pacing adequate to integrating small details, the texture of visual and gestural evocations. The tempo allowed for chance discovery, for the unexpected, to occur within the frame. Time was a key compositional element—time as languid with Nicolás's camera as witness, not voyeur.

We extended these same principles to the subsequent scripting of the film, its structure, editing, and soundscape. At this stage we supplemented observation with the excavation and invention aspects of critique to which Foucault points. Elements from different representational traditions built a visuality of, and from, the sensual beauty of objects, bodies, presences. We edited the segments into a gradually unfolding meditation on desire. The intention was to draw individual performances into a loosely woven narrative that extended their meaning while retaining their discrete character. We did not abandon the observational principle; it guided Nicolás's crafting of a sound design intended to augment the performances, sensorially enhance referential plurality, and give depth and dimension to the additional narrative track I wrote, which comprised dialogue, poetry, text, and prayer.

The narration embeds the performances in a set of exchanges on desire between two voices, Ananya and the Wise One. Their dialogue is intended to frame the performances like lightweight scaffolding, so that the latter may, in Foucault's terms, be their own "signs of life." The performances do not illustrate the conversation between Ananya and the Wise One, though their interplay enables a broader consideration of desire. In response to the question that opens the film—Can you tell me what desire is?—the Wise One instructs Ananya to "sit close and observe," a reworking for our image-oriented present of the ancient adage "sit close and listen," which is also the etymology of *Upanishad*, texts considered to contain the spiritual essence of Hinduism. The offscreen spectator is thus positioned to witness in a double sense. This idea of a frame within a frame is extended to the visual aesthetic of the work.

Witnessing as understood in contemplative practice informs *De Sidere 7* formally and conceptually. In meditative practice, to witness is to become slowly, unresistingly conscious of what shapes perception. One observes the flow of thoughts, feelings, and sensations, and in the same breath witnesses oneself as the observer, becoming aware of all that has formed one's understanding. This dynamic of a continual attentiveness that is at the same time a practice of critical self-reflexivity invites its own formal expression.

It calls for an aesthetic of sensory plenitude that is absorbing without being so immersive as to preclude the possibility of spectatorship as discernment. It requires drawing on the unparalleled capacity of the moving image to conjure sentience, but in a manner that steps away from visual logics that run counter to the expansive, relational, cognitive-experiential intimacy we wished to convey. We sought an aesthetic that positioned the spectator in a relation of intimate remove from the sensory fullness of the work, enabled to observe even while experiencing and vice versa. Spectatorship-as-witnessing further affirmed our decision to draw on a range of representational forms, to develop a structure that could move between different kinds of sensuality and desire, narrativity and abstraction.

We describe *De Sidere 7* as an ensemble videocontemplation. The word *ensemble* is from the Latin *insimul*, in and at the same time. In addition to its musical sense, it means shared space, elements connected by a series of relations, each part being considered only in relation to the whole. *Ensemble* succinctly sums up the effort to construct a work of nonimmersive sensory plenitude situated on the cusp of the inner and the outer and composed of discrete stories that retain their autonomy when inserted into a narrative whole that is greater than the sum of its parts. It speaks to the form of the work. *Videocontemplation* points to our thinking about spectatorship; our intent to position the viewer in a dual relationship of intimacy and remove, enabled to observe even while being drawn into the narrative arc of the work.

six ▼ intimate stranger

You are not your body!
Your body   not you
Your body   not *you*?
Body   are you not   you   me?

An intimate stranger
A dwelling unfamiliar
Unruly matter in need of control
The ground of our being an affront to our senses
Though senses can call only body their home

Blood, breath, and poetry
Pulsing vitality
To taste, touch, and smell
to hear, to behold
the fragrance of colors
the shape of ideas
textured sensations
our pleasures are tactile
So why the delusion of a self d i s embodied
weightlessly skimming, primed to resisting
the layers and flavors of human emotions
and all that enlivens our very existence

seven ▼ tantra and the body

BREATHING IN, we know we are alive. Breathing out, we know we are alive. As long as breath circulates and oxygenates the blood, the rhythm of life is sustained. Inspiration: literally, in breath. In and from the beginning, the indivisibility of body-mind, of physicality and consciousness. If love is the first cause of Creation, tantra is its first effect. Self-other-connectivity. Self-other-divinity. Tantra honors matter, sentience in all its forms. As a path it is anchored in the body: practitioners learn to draw on and from the sensorium in aligning themselves to the nature of Creation as nonhierarchical polyexistence characterized by dense interrelations. "This is like this because that is like that," as the Buddhist notion of dependent co-arising describes it. There is no hierarchy in Creation; hierarchy is a human invention, a terrible innovation.

The COVID-19 pandemic has been an object lesson for a humanity that has acted as though it is separable from nature. All of a sudden it was not just the earth that was struggling to breathe, given our destruction of its lungs, the forests. Not just those living in dangerously polluted cities. All across the world, those infected with the novel coronavirus were gasping for breath. Multiple, overlapping interrelations: these facts of nature imply that human indifference and violence against nature, and against other humans deemed dispensable, cannot but have consequences for each of us, for all of us. Whether or not we personally lived on that basis, whether or not we were responsible for the wrongdoing. We don't need to turn for an explanation to the so-called wrath of God or take a crime-and-punishment approach to the idea of karma. The laws of nature suffice as explanation. "This is like this because that is like that."

The body occupies a paradoxical place in contemporary consumer culture. It is the privileged site of desire and desirability. Alongside and simultaneously, it is the locus of anxiety, disappointment, instability: always threatening to "let one down," seemingly ever in need of "improvement." Natural processes such as aging or unforeseen events like an injury or illness can provoke distaste, even terror. The body becomes something to be endured; if possible, manipulated. Ambivalence and disrespect haunt this conception, compounding a long-prevailing religious suspicion of the body as the site of wayward impulses in need of being disciplined by a focused, unwavering mind.

By contrast, tantra understands the body as a form of intelligence. Tantra proposes that intelligence is triadic: the intelligence of the body, the intelligence of the heart, the intelligence of the mind. All three are necessary. Today, the mind is deemed the primary and undisputed seat of intelligence. In some disciplines and areas of life, the heart's wisdom is accepted. But with signal exceptions, as in the somatic and movement arts, the body remains shrouded in suspicion.

In tantra the body is not the object of practice but rather its subject and its ground. This view flows from the premise of an indivisibility of body-mind and, before that, from tantra's honoring of sentience. The word *sentience* unites aliveness, feeling, and perception. To be alive is to know; to feel is to perceive. The dual meaning of the word *sense* as feeling and as knowledge illustrates this point. And yet the elevation of mind has led to the eclipse of the body as teacher and of the heart as knower.

Tantra does not see the body's intelligence as uncomplicatedly available to the practitioner. It distinguishes between the body itself, which is unconditioned, and our ideas about the body, which are complexly conditioned. To enable the body to be a teacher, then, requires us to confront the tapestry of social conditioning that mediates our relationship to it. But even before we embark on this arduous task of disentanglement, we notice in plain sight a clue to the unconditioned nature of the body: it is virtually impossible to conjure past physical pain. Mental and emotional pain, by contrast, can be triggered again without much effort at all. The body lives only in the present. If some aspect is in pain or discomfort, the body readily expresses it. But when the experience dissolves or passes, the body does not cling to it. Mind and heart, on the other hand, are not solely in the present but equally entangled in past and future. When we speak of bodily memory, then, we are excavating the sedimentation in the body of the experience of mind and heart. Let us note that mind and heart are also *in* the body, pointing to the insufficiency of language in naming interlinked but distinct dimensions of a single whole.

Tantra is a practice of attunement: a form of deep listening, seeing, feeling, touching, tasting, sensing. We gradually discover that each of our faculties is a potential teacher and a portal to understanding, especially if our learning from them proceeds in tandem with the work of deconditioning ourselves. This openness extends to all matter. The world is alive and in conversation. We need only to learn how to hear, what to listen for. Slowing down and observing closely, listening within listening, feeling within feeling, and so on. Like a sculptor learning from clay; the gardener, from plants; or the musician, from the interval between notes.

COVID-19 compelled a reckoning with our disdain for physicality and matter. We have valued so-called mental labor over physical labor (so-called because no work is not at once both physical and mental). And yet this crisis forced us to recognize as essential the labor of those who are the least paid and least valued, those working in agriculture, sanitation, trash collection, grocery stores, transportation, restaurant and food delivery, domestic and care work—the informal sectors of the economy. And given the logic of maximizing profits that shapes every sector, it turns out that even doctors in the US were subordinate to hospital administrators with MBAs, compelled to reuse personal protective equipment and substitute garbage bags for surgical gowns. Meanwhile, those who had been habituated to contracting out cooking, cleaning, and other such tasks spent unaccustomed hours in undertaking activities essential to reproducing everyday life.

The breathing lung. The beating heart. The pangs of hunger. The pleasures of food preparation. The fear of penury. Relief at a reprieve from the treadmill of work. The precarity of life. The pandemic has been wake-up call (not the first and, regrettably, likely not the last) to remake our unequal societies and the untenable basis on which we have sought to take our place on this planet.

Tantra is an invitation to intimacy with all that exists. It honors the integrity of matter, embodiment, process. Its pedagogy aligns with the laws of nature, with the nature of creation as nonhierarchical interdependence, egalitarian polyexistence. It is one among many originary wisdoms that speak directly to us as we seek a new equilibrium, one that rests in a realization of the indivisible whole of which we are a part. A whole from which all things arise. In which all things exist. And to which all things return.

eight ▼
to
bend
into
the
wind

FRAGILITY, N.

A QUALITY **INTRINSIC** TO ALL THAT EXISTS

TO INTERDEPENDENT
IMPERMANENCE

NOT WEAKNESS OR BROKENNESS
BUT A FORM **OF COMPLEXITY**

TO **RESIST** IT
AS FOOLISH
AS REJECTING GRAVITY

WWW.THEPOETICSOFFRAGILITY.COM

Fragility poster, 2016. Design by Nicolás Grandi, Lata Mani, and Bharath Haridas.

NOTA BENE

A praise song is not a privileging
but a reclamation, a reckoning
a *cri de coeur*, a primal scream
an observing, an honoring

the hues, the tones, the *bhava*
the melody, the *rasa*
the aria, the plainchant
the ragas of states of mind

such particulars compose
the music of experience
to reject, pay no heed to them
would neglect, deflect our humanness

to open on the other hand
to the gifts that our undoing brings
is to stay the course with grace and grit
to activate the alchemist

"Nota Bene," Nicolás Grandi and Lata Mani, 2021.

NOTA BENE: A SUTRA IN FOUR SCENES

Shadow Puppet Video Installation

With Nicolás Grandi and Tolubommalata Master Puppeteers Shinde
Anjaneyulu and Family

HD, 2021, 8:25 MINUTES

https://doi.org/10.6084/m9.figshare.17018594

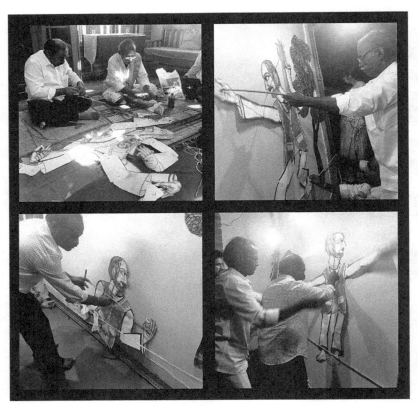

Shinde Anjaneyalu and Shinde Maruthi Rao on the set of "Nota Bene," 2018.

nine ▾ love is not a state of exception

IT SEEMS AS THOUGH we already know what love is. And yet a lot can be said about love, about what it has come to mean and what it could mean, about its simultaneously self-evident and enigmatic character. Love is a stable resting place and a state of flux. As the former it can be a point of anchorage; as the latter—as yearning that eludes fulfillment or unfolds in ways that slip away from one's grasp—love is a source of disturbance and anxiety.

Those of a spiritual or religious persuasion consider the universe to manifest the love of its Creator. One may or may not accept this premise. But is it not intriguing that the nature of love and the nature of life have so much in common, suggesting at the very least that love is primordial?

Love and life are both inherently relational, complexly interconnected processes. Both involve dynamic and evolving relationships of interdependence, negotiation, adaptation, cooperation, conflict, struggle. Both require discovery and learning, not just about self but equally about other—indeed, about countless others. Both equally imply unlearning. In love, as in life, one can look in the mirror of self and find wisdom as well as delusion. One bows before love just as one bows before life, open, curious, expectant.

Neither love nor life is at root a "thing," a mere concept. Both love and life are experiences. To say this is not to say that there is no conceptual thinking about either. Concepts are the building blocks of cognition: we think with and through them. So it is that shifting ideas about love shape our perception and experience. But that is not all. As has happened innumerable times in history, our experience of love has breached the then prevailing languages of love, affirming new longings, birthing other ecstasies.

Love is not a freestanding entity but an active state of being. To love is to be in relationship; not in *a* relationship but *in relationship*. Love is in that sense more verb than noun. The same is true of life.

Love's elemental nature is manifest in how it simultaneously activates mind, heart, and body. Love is at once idea, emotion, and physical sensation. Any notion of love that disarticulates this triadic relationship drains love of its fullness and denies that which constitutes our very embodiment. It renders love a ghostly shadow of itself.

Love is not an obligation. Duty and command have no claim on love, though both pretend otherwise. Love conjugates itself with fearlessness, vulnerability, and clear seeing. It is a commitment to discovering the truth(s) of relationality and in that context the ethic of one's responsibility and response-ability.

Such a process is by its very nature open-ended, with no guarantees and no terminus. We can only prepare for it by remaining open, just as when love arrives unbidden and dissolves imagined futures. Love, like life, is lit by spontaneity, expectation, discovery, cultivation, joy, grief, and unknowing. Love is not a state of exception.

The dharma or ethic of love is distorted when specific kinds of love—of parent, partner, spouse, child, family—insist on asserting unique privileges. But if love is not a state of exception, on what grounds would particular kinds of love claim special entitlements? To stake a special claim is to contest the idea of love as freedom to discover the truths of relationality.

This definition recognizes the centrality of free will to love. Love cannot be commandeered into existence or dismissed by fiat. To enforce love or to discipline its circulation is to violate its nature as a species of the freedom to seek truth. At the same time, by placing relationality at the center of the pursuit of truth, this formulation sets aside an individualistic conception of self. It conceives of the individual as a node in a web of nature-culture interrelations. As a node the individual is not separable from the web. Rather she/he/they is/are the continual distillation of an evolving engagement with relationality, the sum of its effects. Love is at once cause, energizing force, and consequence of this process.

chapter nine

As cause and dynamizing force, love can shatter existing frames of reference and self-understandings. That said, individual experience is more commonly shaped by the cluster of ideas and assumptions that characterize a historical moment. The journey to truth necessarily traverses the minefield of social conditioning, and love in the expansive sense described here is a frequent casualty. "Radicalism" is too often content with a politics of antithesis, with simply inverting the discourse of conservatism. Love is thus corralled into small enclosures of competing conventionalisms, prevented from renewing itself and all those who long for it.

Iterations of love are inescapably individual and inevitably transpersonal. This is life on/as a node. Love, with a capital *L*, does not hover over us waiting to pronounce judgment with a clap of thunder and a bolt of lightning. And it has sent to earth no special forces to keep us in line.

The Creator as a punitive, authoritarian overlord is an empty projection. Free will implies its own pedagogy: incremental, tentative, dialogical, dialectical, an evolving synthesis. We are spider and spittle, weaver and woven, the node and the weave.

ten ▼ california poppy

one California poppy
can stop a day in its tracks
its nectarous orange
pulsing for hours
in one's consciousness

eleven ▼ "a glorious thing made up of stardust"

WHAT PAT PARKER & ROHITH VEMULA ASK US TO CONSIDER

The first thing you do is to forget that I'm black.
Second, you must never forget that I'm black.
—PAT PARKER, "For the White Person
Who Wants to Know How to Be My Friend"

IN THESE OPENING LINES OF HER POEM, "For the White Person Who Wants to Know How to Be My Friend," Pat Parker names a paradox at the heart of challenging socially produced difference. Parker is speaking not to diversity *in* nature, nor to the diversity *of* nature. Not to the variations of appearance (size, shade, height, foliage, texture) or mode of expression (hoot, howl, accent, gesture, cultural practices). Her lines address a uniquely human phenomenon: prejudice. They speak to the poignant difficulty of challenging a spurious and malevolent construction of racial difference in a society still in the grip of its miasma.

I have recalled Parker's lines many times in the days of sorrow, tumult, and righteous rage that followed Rohith Vemula's suicide. Rohith Vemula was a scholar and activist who took his own life on January 17, 2016, after months of harassment by the University of Hyderabad for his work toward an expansive, inclusive, and just society. His death sparked nationwide protests against caste discrimination that is entrenched in education and the systematic suppression of dissent as "antinational." "Rohith Vemula's suicide." I am holding off from saying "Dalit scholar Rohith Vemula's suicide." Or, as is now being said with good reason, "Dalit scholar Rohith Vemula's institutional murder." I defer by a couple of sentences a description of him that refers to the caste into which he was born, to honor if only symbolically his anguish that the contingent facts of his birth had indelibly defined his life. He was twenty-six years old at the time of his death.

▼

How do we acknowledge the quotidian and institutionalized violence of race, caste, or any socially sanctioned form of discrimination in contexts defined by their simultaneous avowal and disavowal? By documenting, narrating, and insisting on their reality. By drawing out the multiplicity of causes and effects that the forked tongue of dominant discourse elides, denies, or rewrites as pathology and lack. By turning the discourse of the privileged on its head, pointing to the lies that sustain it and the refusals in which it is founded. "Never forget that I'm black." This we have substantial experience in doing. And we do it well: not only those who are subject to discrimination but also many among the privileged who are committed to social justice. Academic and activist research, investigative journalism, and reports from fact-finding commissions, governments, and other groups attest to a well-developed documentary tradition.

But what about, "forget that I'm black"? The first injunction calls for something else, hints at something other. It asks one to see anew. Take note of what we seem to notice and to think about what we make of it; look again at what we tend to overlook and ask why. Look. Again. Think. Rethink.

"Forget that I'm black." At first blush it seems to address the privileged. "You who see me solely as X or Y, think again!" But it could be said to equally address those hemmed in by a given social description. It is Parker speaking of herself, to the fact that her life exceeds the categories that supposedly render it intelligible. She is reminding us that one is more than the sum of reigning social descriptions. One is other than; one is also-and. One is *not* that/not *just* that/also *yes, that!*, and far, far more besides.

Rohith Vemula's suicide note states it eloquently: "The value of a man was reduced to his immediate identity and nearest possibility. To a vote.

To a number. To a thing. Never was a man treated as a mind. As a glorious thing made up of stardust. In every field, in studies, in streets, in politics, and in dying and living" (Vemula 2016).

Given the necessity to insist "never forget that I'm ____," we can easily overlook the warning Parker embeds in her call to "forget that I'm black." Speaking truth to miasma involves a terrible burden. We are required to repeat its lies in order to establish their continued social circulation. Critique and its object are always necessarily in dialogue. Consequently, every repetition invokes not merely the fact of injustice but also the sense of diminishment, the pain of discrimination. To speak to/of miasma involves temporarily inhabiting its lies, embodying them as speech. The effects are searing, acidic, toxic.

Resistance is often imagined as acting against an external force or edifice. But this outward motion is only one aspect of a process that continually returns us to ourselves. We are located within the structures we seek to dismantle. They inhabit us as much as we inhabit them. We may be differentially positioned within them and manifest varying degrees of awareness about them. But each of us is on the inside. Indeed, part of our work is that of insisting on each of us belonging, on all of our "insiderness," even as we propose to reimagine the republic and our interrelationships.

To do battle with a miasma is to wrestle with a delusory and illusory mode of perception. Illusion: seeing what is not there. Delusion: a misperception that has crossed over into psyche. To do battle with the miasma of caste or race is to simultaneously hold in one's consciousness a challenging amalgam of truth and falsehood, fact and fiction: lies about caste/race, facts regarding their brutal persistence, and the truth that these categories can never adequately express the rich actuality or fullness of who one is. It is a tall order. The wear and tear on psyche, body, mind, and heart can be insuperable.

Perhaps it is to this inner battle that Rohith refers when he writes, "I feel a growing gap between my soul and my body. And I have become a monster" (Vemula 2016). Holding steadfastly to truth in the face of continual lies and harassment had produced in him a sense of alienation from self. The feeling that he had become something other than himself distressed him and compounded a prior loneliness.

Social justice discourse is structured by the dialectic of negation and assertion. Every negation is itself a form of assertion, every assertion an implicit negation. But despite the fluid, evolving, and multiplicitous character of life—and by extension, of resistance to how society deems it should be lived—social resistance frequently tends to manifest as a binary force, not a multilateral one. This is even more so when opposition is directed toward apparatuses of the state, the arbiter of social life in our times. This *tendency* to binarism cannot make room for the kind of complex simultaneity of negation-assertion invoked in Parker's invitation to "forget" and to "never forget." It cannot facilitate acknowledging negative social ascription in a way that centers the vibrant richness of the lives and life-worlds of those discriminated.

To the contrary. The facts of discrimination become the motor of social justice rhetoric. It is as though the lives being defended are comprehensible within its terms and containable by them. The inertia of the tendency generates a discursive continuum whose two end points are victimization and liberation. The former temporally signifies past/present; the latter, a present/future to be galvanized via individual and collective agency. This narrative reduces life to the logic of social ascription. It accords precedence to prevailing structures of power over the human capacity to creatively resist even under dire circumstances. In so doing it diminishes the multidimensionality of what it means to live under the sign of a negative social ascription, to be dalit or black or _____. Activists fighting social exclusion on behalf of themselves and their communities face a peculiar predicament. The critique of social exclusion can itself contribute, if only inadvertently, to a sense of alienation from self.

What can social justice discourse do to ameliorate the trauma wrought by the need to engage with the falsehoods of miasma? It can more fully commit itself to an affirmative discourse that goes beyond the language of rights denied and of cultures of resistance, for these continue to place structures of power at the center. These concerns can be reframed within a broader consideration of the life-worlds and practices—cultural, ethical, aesthetic, and philosophical—that give meaning and texture to the everyday lives of individuals and communities deemed marginal by the social order.

Power may cast a long shadow, but except in its own imagination, it is not the sole actor or determinant. There are many dimensions that lie beyond its reach, others that retain a degree of autonomy and still others in which power is navigated, negotiated, ignored, and challenged in small and not-so-small ways: through noncooperation, wit, paradoxical thinking, and counternarratives that invert and rewrite the sociocultural script. Expanding the frame in the way suggested here will ensure a fuller, more balanced perspective.

It will also relieve activists from a narrative whose burden many find too heavy to bear, one in which heroic social activism is made responsible for slaying the shame-dragon of social ascription. Given the sorry state of human affairs, victory can seem distant and unreachable. The ensuing sorrow, rage, and despair can congeal into depression and hopelessness. The biographical, social, institutional, and political can fold in upon each other. Finding it difficult to keep going, some have taken their lives.

It takes more than a discursive shift to resolve social problems. But our rhetoric and framework can either nourish our capacity to stay the course or else unintentionally serve to inhibit it. Addressing social problems involves analyzing each oppressive detail even while looking beyond their constricting view toward the expansive horizon of freedom. The social critic or activist confronts a problem that contemplative traditions would pose as that of "how to touch the story of suffering." Perhaps this question, along with Parker's twinned instructions to "forget," "never forget," can serve as a kind of koan upon which we might reflect in seeking another way forward.

twelve ▼ benediction

May grief be a benediction that cleanses and renews
For it is an honoring of self
Individual   collective
A determination to bear witness to love
in the face of all that appears to mock, taunt, diminish, and dispirit
And when it passes   as it will
May you be replenished
And glisten like a spider's web after a storm

thirteen ▼ objects in the mirror are closer than you think

BEYOND THE RHETORIC OF OTHERNESS

POLITICAL DISCOURSE in the contemporary period is marked by an affective intensity. Regardless of the issue, an acute depth of feeling is evident. Righteousness, betrayal, entitlement, anguish, and aggression suffuse arguments across the political spectrum. What seems to be at stake is the desire not merely to speak but to have the terms of one's discourse deemed legitimate, to be understood as one understands oneself. The sizzle, crack, and snap of rhetoric expresses the heightened temperature. One could credibly interpret it as the sound of an existing order breaking down under multiple pressures. This explanation would, however, be a partial one. The surcharged atmosphere is equally evidence of the ties that bind those who passionately disagree with each other. And therein lies a clue.

The politics of liberation in "societies structured in dominance" (Hall 1980) partly entails the effort to distinguish between diversity as a form of natural variation and difference that is socially produced. Put another way, it involves learning to differentiate between difference conceived as "otherness," carrying values assigned to it by the prevailing social order, and difference understood as a kind of specificity that exists in context of an interdependent diversity. Prevailing conceptions of gender, race, caste, and sexuality are examples of socially produced difference, difference as otherness. The diversity of plants, shrubs, trees, grasses are instances of difference conceived as specificity, a benign variation that manifests the play of interdependent diversity.

The two conceptions are not discontinuous. Otherness is most often produced through a negative and hostile evaluation of specificity on the spurious grounds that it diverges from or threatens a prevailing norm and must therefore be policed, domesticated, or subordinated. A politics of liberation could have refused this distinction. It could have insisted that difference as otherness must in all instances cede ground to difference as specificity, as throughout the rest of nature. But with the exception of indigenous movements, whose histories require a different mapping, that has not been the direction taken. For the most part, political movements have chosen to reclaim otherness, to resignify its meaning, to challenge the identification of particular characteristics with specific groups, and to broaden the range of cultural, sexual, bodily, and identitarian differences to which we must attend if we are to embrace a truly inclusive vision of liberation.

That this strategy became—and remains—the preferred approach is not surprising. Post-Enlightenment thinking proposed a sharp divergence between humans and the rest of nature. Humans were held to be superior and other to the natural world of which they were a part. A part, yet apart. Bounded, autonomous entities possessing a singular awareness and agency, self-willed humans stood in stark contrast with the rest of nature, which was construed as inert matter uniquely subject to its environment (broadly understood) and a resource with which we could do as we pleased. The extraction of humans from our place in nature facilitated our exploitation of nature. That said, difference in the nonhuman natural world was understood as the effect of irreducibly complex evolutionary processes that were multifaceted, transspecies, and interlinked. This enabling notion of difference—as a kind of specificity expressing complex and multiple interdependencies—made diversity in the nonhuman natural world a source of endless aesthetic pleasure and scientific curiosity, not to mention spiritual succor. Might radical politics stand to gain by extending this notion of difference to the human realm?

▼

chapter thirteen

Dominant ideology interprets concepts and social relations in accordance with its own logic. The axes along which it divides and the hierarchies it proposes as legitimate vary depending on context. But most frequently at the heart of such maneuvers to exclude or oppress are gender, sexuality, ethnicity, religion, and, when pertinent, race, caste, and tribe. The history of such contentions and their consequences is complex, the subject of extensive scholarship. But one recurrent strategy has been to invent the lie of otherness via the so-called truths of history, science, biology, or religion, which are often deployed in some combination.

Regardless of the particularities of a given lie, such "othering" produced a state of estrangement. It rendered concepts, peoples, and social relations other than what they are. One does not need to subscribe to a golden age theory of the past to consider what I am saying here. To mark out a difference is to intervene. It is a deliberate act and an act of deliberation. It suggests something being made, remade, made up even. In any event, it inaugurates a shift whose contemporary forms and reverberations we inherit. And it is these that are challenged in current struggles for justice.

Arguments for equality generally both point to similarity and insist on difference. Sometimes this approach involves reclaiming a difference that had been disparaged (black is beautiful) at other times rejection of it (the association of purity with a particular caste or race). At yet other times, the category is itself made incoherent, as with gender after the emergence of the movement for transgender rights. Pressured to accommodate so much diversity, gender risks imploding. What kind of difference does gender make? What kinds of genders does difference make? Add to gender nonconformism the proliferations of sexualities, and matters become even more complex.

As always, contradictory dynamics are simultaneously in play: an expansion and a consolidation. As conventional understandings of gender come under intense pressure, they can gain traction in the medical and psychological literature, for example, the idea of gender dysmorphia, a misalignment between one's sense of one's gender identity and the gender that would customarily be attributed to one's physical body. Gender-nonconforming persons can be required to ground claims about their true gender identity in conventional notions, even as their ways of embodying gender can stretch it beyond recognition. By way of example, consider a transwoman who has declined hormones and surgery and opted to keep their beard and move through the world wearing women's clothing. Law may have created a third gender, but the binary haunts the route to reclassification, as if transgender were a space holder for gender migrants who can expect to be denied full citizenship in the gender(s) of their choosing. The binary is dead; long live the binary.

So long as difference is understood as otherness, proliferation and consolidation will feed each other and keep the norm dynamically intact, even while instigating impassioned counterdiscourse on the uniquely particular or exceptional nature of the experience of a given gender, caste, sexuality, race, ethnicity, religion, or tribe. The two processes are activated in tandem. The violence of othering initiates a hardening of categories and stances. It inclines us to talk at and past each other. Our mutual ignorance (at times incomprehension) becomes a confirming sign of the incommensurability of our experiences. We confront each other as distressed opponents across the divides of past and present injustices. The ensuing pain and antagonism are seen to vitiate the atmosphere, making dialogue impossible. But there is more to be noticed. The emotional pitch also testifies to the intimacy of this standoff. This aspect begs our attention.

▼

Othering is a strategy of power. It distorts complexity. It denies relationality. It asserts a hierarchy. Complex wholes are fragmented. Entities and processes that have evolved in multiplicitous contexts and interrelationships are deemed radically separable, wholly autonomous. Or else as existing only in the relationship of subordination proposed by the logic of otherness. Certain modes of understanding gender, race, and caste may be located here.

Concepts are not the world but an attempt to describe it. The world precedes and exceeds them, and it cannot be simplified by dint of will. Discourse about the world is thus intrinsically vulnerable to disputation, permanently unsettled. Difference as otherness is at odds with the heterogeneous complexity of the social world. The affective intensity of our debates is a sign of this. It registers a kind of intuitive discomfort with the idea of otherness even as it is being deployed. It is discursive static overlying the pulse of all that is suppressed, all that can at any time erupt and disrupt the arguments being made.

Difference as specificity within interdependent diversity is a much more capacious and flexible conception, one that offers the added benefit of not carrying the burden of an a priori value judgment. It enables one to analyze social variation in all its *multiconstitutedness*. In an interdependent universe, everything emerges out of relationality and exists *as* relationality. Relatedness is a fact of nature and the grounding truth of sociality. To posit difference as otherness is to refuse to integrate this reality, to wittingly or unwittingly collude in its distortion. Any ideology or perspective that segments, separates, divides, and hierarchizes individuals, communities, or experiences obscures this first principle.

Regardless of what supremacists might falsely claim about gender, caste, race, sexuality, or religion, we are a complexly interconnected diversity, mutually and multiply constituted in relation to each other and all that exists, human and nonhuman. Segregation spatializes some people's fear of proximity, contamination, and pollution. But it does not alter the fundamental truth of mutuality, which is why such elaborate and violent mechanisms are needed in order to enforce the lie of hierarchy and separateness. And why the assertion of essential difference is less threatening to supremacists of all stripes than insistence on intersectionality, inextricability, and syncretism.

Our lives are composed of myriad intimacies. Yet we experience these as so many estrangements, antagonisms, and irrelevances. To speak of equality is to tacitly acknowledge multiplicity and relationality: equality is always with-within-among-between-across. But we are yet to embrace the full implications of this fact, which is why we can so easily take recourse to a rhetoric of otherness or position ourselves outside the structures of which we are a part, no matter how differentially we may be located within them.

But there is no outside. There is no other. There is only intimacy. It may be denied, resisted, violated, distorted, or celebrated. It may be eclipsed by our indifference, inattention, and ignor(e)ance. Still, it is here, awaiting language adequate to its truths.

fourteen ▼ *words fall into empty mind*
with nicolás grandi

HD, 2015, 1.09 MINUTES

"Words Fall into Empty Mind,"
Nicolás Grandi and Lata Mani, 2015.

https://doi.org/10.6084/m9.figshare.17018591

fifteen ▼ does the mind have a heart?

A TICKER TAPE OF EVENTS, opinions, experiences, and facts (real and invented) stream ceaselessly in our direction. The air is thick with them. The stories of manifold others distant and proximate give shape to our days. And yet these lives remain at once familiar and strange to us, intimate and alien. Names, dates, atrocities, facts, figures, persons loom large and then disappear in the clamor of subsequent events. The detritus accumulates in our minds like improvised explosive devices waiting to be tripped. What will it take for our consciousness to detonate?

"These kinds of questions are not the ones to ask," sighs Nadia Murad, when reflecting on being repeatedly asked to narrate the details of the sexual violence she endured while she was held captive by ISIS. "The things I want to be asked are, 'What must be done so Yazidis can have their rights? What must be done so a woman will not be a victim of war?' These are the kinds of things I want to be asked more often."

Murad continued this theme in her December 15, 2016, address to the United Nations. "Today I'm not only talking on my behalf—about what happened to me. Here I am the voice of 3,200 girls, women and children still in captivity. I beg you to put humans first. This life was not only created for you and your families. We also want life and it's our right to live it" (Bombach 2018).

Does the ear have a heart? Can the eye feel?

▼

Denis Mukwege is always patient with interviewers overwhelmed by his accounts of the systematic use of sexual violence against women as a weapon in the conflict in the Democratic Republic of Congo between 1998 and 2003. Unsure how to respond to his distressing revelations, journalists frequently ask him what people should do with this information.

"The main message we must impart is that of peace," he says calmly, "because it is our right." He then proceeds to offer as a kind of implicit example his own relationship with the women to whom he is doctor, pastor, and friend: "I identify every woman raped with my wife. I identify every mother raped with my own mother. Every child raped with my children" (Mukwege 2016). Without saying so explicitly, Mukwege invites us to do the same. The women and children are kin, not Other, to him.

Like countless individuals who have needed to plumb the depths of their own humanity in the context of unspeakable violence, Mukwege and Murad are acutely aware that they are holding a mirror to *us*. In pleading for our attention, they implore us to embrace the true measure of what it means to be fully human, understanding that *our* humanity is at stake in our silence, incomprehension, or inaction. To not limit our responseability to awarding them prizes even while ignoring the issues they so poignantly raise.

▼

It is often remarked that we live in an age of heightened emotion. Feelings are customarily associated with the heart. But the affective intensity we witness today is predominantly that of the mind. Rage, frustration, and hate are the province of mind. When the mind is primary and centrally involved, feeling and knowing converge and collapse one into the other. This convergence undermines the ability of heart to act as foil, check, or counterpoint to mind. Depth of feeling itself becomes evidence for the "truth" of convictions. Those in this state refuse to countenance evidence that challenges their view, or else they deny and distort the arguments of opponents.

Conflicts around existing social faultlines devolve into bitter contestations over "knowledge," "history," "culture," "truth." And violence is justified as a means of settling disagreements and disputes.

To the heart is given love, joy, and grief. Love and joy are expansive and hopeful, whereas grief constricts and at times paralyzes. Love and joy inspire generosity, unlike the aggressive defensiveness characteristic of the inflamed mind. Indeed, the liquification of heart in love or joy soothes the mind. It is literally impossible to be happy and angry at the same time. And although grief may temporarily exile hope, it rarely leads to aggression—unless it is grossly neglected, repressed, and denied, whether by an individual or by society. At which point it can morph into rage and set the mind on fire.

The heart is not, however, merely the seat of feelings. It is also a form of intelligence. If only mind would listen. Does the mind have a heart?

Murad and Mukwege ask us to apply our mind and open our hearts to the suffering of others. To make the connection between rape as a tool of terror in the scramble for minerals in the Congo, and our use of the cell phones for which those minerals are mined. To put ourselves in the shoes of those under the reign of terror that ISIS unleashed on Yazidis and others subject to their rule. If we are to respond to their call, we must open not only our hearts. Nor only our minds. We must learn to discern the mind of heart and simultaneously to feel the heart of mind.

sixteen ▼ sticks and stones
may break my bones . . . but words?

ON SOCIAL JUSTICE RHETORIC

When people speak about this or that, I try to imagine what the result would be if translated into reality. When they "criticize" someone, when they "denounce" his ideas, when they "condemn" what he writes, I imagine them in the ideal situation in which they would have complete power over him. I take the words they use—demolish, destroy, reduce to silence, bury—and see what the effect would be if taken literally.
—MICHEL FOUCAULT, "The Masked Philosopher"

FOUCAULT'S WORDS ARE unsettlingly apposite to the political climate in India after 2014, when an authoritarian government sought to quite literally crush and eliminate all dissent, all dissenters, any notion it deemed illegitimate. The totalitarian fantasies of the Bharatiya Janata Party and its affiliates give us a real-time view of the violence that Foucault's words can only discursively conjure. It gives us pause to think about a tendency in the rhetorical practices of social justice activism, one not specific to India alone.

Activists express social justice concerns by means of several genres: position papers, legal briefs, fact-finding reports, press releases, scholarly essays, poetry, songs, slogans, first-person accounts, analytical blogs, and opinion pieces. Each genre offers its own tonal range in what is expressible and by extension audible. Argument, polemic, report, or testimonial can combine reason, passion, wit, rage, hope, grief, love, frustration, and disbelief. Some iterations abbreviate complexity into finely honed rhetorical screams. Others artfully extend the formal constraints of a given genre to create the unexpected. On occasion, an inspired slogan can condense the core idea and zeitgeist of a movement. "We are the 99%" or "Black Lives Matter" are recent examples, as is "Jai Bhim, Lal Salaam," which sums up the yearning for a more egalitarian coming-together of Indian Left and Dalit movements during the current phase of the struggle against casteism, social inequality, and freedom of thought and expression.

The plurality of forms and affects makes sociopolitical critique a vibrant and diverse space. That said, the not-uncommon tendency to adopt an oppositional mode of address makes such critique vulnerable to enacting the kind of violence Foucault describes. It is not surprising that some might assume such a stance. After all, social justice activism is a form of protest, a boundary-pushing activity. It is concerned with unfinished business: social norms that contravene law, rights usurped or never conferred, varieties of social inequality and exclusion, the unequal apportionment of state resources, and so on. It frequently addresses the state and its institutions. In such a context one can come to think of the marshaling of word-image-sound as akin to hurling semiotic bricks against prevailing structures of power. It is thus that, regardless of genre, a strong undercurrent of polemic is to be found.

Polemic derives from *polemos*, the Greek word for war. It refers to a strongly worded argument against an opposing perspective. In describing *polemic* in this way, I have deliberately excluded three terms also customarily used in defining it: *aggressive, attack, controversial.* The last of these relates to the context of theological debate, which is not relevant here; the first two I have rephrased as "strongly worded" so that we may think about how to retain the vigor of such a mode of disputation without taking on the aggression implied by its etymological root in the Greek word for war. The opposite of *polemic* is *irenic*, deriving from *eirenikos*, the Greek word for peace. In Greek mythology, Eirene is one of the goddesses of the seasons and the natural order. *Irenics* is defined as a conciliatory mode of engagement, pacific, nonpolemical; in the theological context it presents points of agreement among Christians to emphasize their ultimate unity. If we bracket the sense of irenics as a mode of subsuming difference in the interest of unity but hold to the ideas of peace and the natural order of things, we can draw on both polemic and irenic to reconsider some of our rhetoric.

It could be argued that the scale and depth of prevailing injustice warrant retaining aggression as integral to polemic. Such a view, however, makes little sense given that the goal of activism is to re-create society, enable a new mode of relating to one another. Activism is the praxis of persuasion, the remaking of social norms through cumulative collective action until even those who continue to resist recognize their position to be socially illegitimate. It is a continual process with stops, starts, switchbacks, and reversals. It involves working to dismantle not only external institutional edifices but also the internal cognitive and affective frames that shape our perception of things. The idea of word-image-sound as hurled brick cannot capture this dual movement.

And yet the idea persists among the privileged and the disenfranchised. As rage or grief projected outward. As a way of positioning oneself outside the structure or social faultline under discussion. As a means of challenging a differing point of view. As a way of proclaiming innocence of intention. Propelled at times by the added velocity of a sense of superiority, whether inherited as social capital or claimed as a right denied. As a consequence, rhetoric about violence can itself become belligerent, even mobilizing denunciation and shame. Such a strategy cannot persuade anyone who does not already agree with us, though such individuals might feel affirmed by what we say, perhaps even by how we say it.

One reason this mode of address seems legitimate is that activist discourse, for the most part, implicitly or explicitly addresses the state or those implacably opposed to whatever is being argued for, defended, or challenged, or else others in the social justice movement. This tendency effectively overlooks the vast middle of society—the overwhelming majority—that evinces a multiplicity of perspectives and varying degrees of concern and indifference, all of which can be bewildering to the Left and the Right alike, albeit for different reasons. This "middle" largely functions as a kind of backdrop for the pointed volley of arguments between the two organized ends of the continuum. Typically, the Right falsely claims to represent these multitudes, especially in matters of culture, whereas the Left can seem wary of them, a skepticism sometimes misplaced and at other times justified. But no real social transformation is possible without directly addressing this populous segment, and an aggressive approach is unlikely to meet with enthusiastic reception, which is why groups working in and with communities generally adopt a different strategy from activists campaigning about issues.

Far more important, however, than an instrumental concern about what will not work is the truth that social movements are living laboratories of the futures they envisage. How we deal with difference in all its dimensions thus becomes a crucial litmus test, whether we are speaking of difference as in the varieties of social experience that characterize an unequal society or as in differing perspectives regarding the best means of addressing the problems, tensions, and conflicts that ensue. The dynamic of uncompromising opposition needs to be in a continual relationship with an evolving imagination of our post-conflict future. We will have to live alongside and amid those whom we have energetically opposed. Our politics must reflect that reality.

An abiding focus on the state and on law has enabled the self-other binary to persist in social justice discourse. It is as though we can leave to law and a range of institutional mechanisms the management of life after conflict, the work of reconciliation in its sense of "bringing together once again." But the negative restraint of law is useful only if it is supported by an affirmative change of heart among a substantial majority. And that requires a discourse that goes beyond inverting existing hierarchies and their values to reimagining a nonhierarchical means of living our interrelationality. It implies moving away from a conception of society as the agglomeration of distinct collectivities whose relations can be institutionally mediated, toward thinking of personal and social interrelations as forms of dense mutualities.

Interrelationality and mutuality are preconditions of existence, the natural order of things. In that sense both already prevail, though in forms distorted by the hierarchies in place and in play in a given society. In challenging these hierarchies, we tend to reclaim socially produced difference by asserting separateness, in the process downplaying the facts of our complex if unequal interconnectedness. To recenter interrelationality and mutuality would be to pivot political practice. For it would dissolve the self-other binary (a secondary misperception) to lay bare the primary misperception: the disavowal of interrelationship in the production of difference as Otherness.

To work from this basis is to restore intimacy to politics. There is no absolute Other separable from oneself. Both continually constitute each other, though not (yet) in just or egalitarian ways. To take this approach is also to more fully integrate the simultaneously inward-outward dynamic of politics as a transformative process. Such a reorientation would inspire its own rhetoric, one no less vigorous, complex, or compelling, though perhaps less Other-directed and focused equally on the questions of how we are to live together and how we can challenge existing structures of inequality. It would enable a new conjunction of polemic and irenic—hard work, to be sure, but more equal to the hopes and dreams of liberation that fuel activism. For far too long we have allowed the violence of history to shape our imagination of the future, not trusting that we can and must expect more from ourselves, from each other, and from that blessed activity we have come to call "politics."

seventeen ▼ "what i noticed most was that i had become a poet"

RENEWING THE LANGUAGE OF POLITICS

GHAYATH ALMADHOUN'S PROSE POEMS startle with their complexity. Within a few short sentences we are immersed in storylines that we are hard-pressed to explain yet feel familiar in their strangeness. Almadhoun narrates the recognizably contemporary with loving exactitude. But his words read like a prophecy whose meaning we are still to grasp. Ghayath Almadhoun is a Damascus-born Palestinian poet-filmmaker now based in Stockholm.

HOW I BECAME . . .

Her grief fell from the balcony and broke into pieces, so she needed a new grief. When I went with her to the market the prices were unreal, so I advised her to buy a used grief. We found one in excellent condition although it was a bit big. As the vendor told us, it belonged to a young poet who had killed himself the previous summer. She liked this grief so we decided to take it. We argued with the vendor over the price and he said he'd give us an angst dating from the sixties as a free gift if we bought the grief. We agreed, and I was happy with this unexpected angst. She sensed this and said "It's yours." I took it and put it in my bag and we went off. In the evening I remembered it and took it out of the bag and examined it closely. It was high quality and in excellent condition despite half a century of use. The vendor must have been unaware of its value otherwise he wouldn't have given it to us in exchange for buying a young poet's low-quality grief. The thing that pleased me most about it was that it was existentialist angst, meticulously crafted and containing details of extraordinary subtlety and beauty. It must have belonged to an intellectual with encyclopedic knowledge or a former prisoner. I began to use it and insomnia became my constant companion. I became an enthusiastic supporter of peace negotiations and stopped visiting relatives. There were increasing numbers of memoirs in my bookshelves and I no longer voiced my opinion, except on rare occasions. Human beings became more precious to me than nations and I began to feel a general ennui, but what I noticed most was that I had become a poet.

—Ghayath Almadhoun, *Adrenalin*

MASSACRE

Massacre is a dead metaphor that is eating my friends, eating them without salt. They were poets and have become Reporters With Borders; they were already tired and now they're even more tired. "They cross the bridge at daybreak fleet of foot" and die with no phone coverage. I see them through night vision goggles and follow the heat of their bodies in the darkness; there they are, fleeing from it even as they run towards it, surrendering to this huge massage. Massacre is their true mother, while genocide is no more than a classical poem written by intellectual pensioned-off generals. Genocide isn't appropriate for my friends, as it's an organized collective action and organized collective actions remind them of the Left that let them down.

Massacre wakes up early, bathes my friends in cold water and blood, washes their underclothes and makes them bread and tea, then teaches them a little about the hunt. Massacre is more compassionate to my friends than the Universal Declaration of Human Rights. Massacre opened the door to them when other doors were closed, and called them by their names when news reports were looking for numbers. Massacre is the only one to grant them asylum regardless of their backgrounds; their economic circumstances don't bother Massacre, nor does Massacre care whether they are intellectuals or poets, Massacre looks at things from a neutral angle; Massacre has the same dead features as them, the same names as their widowed wives, passes like them through the countryside and the suburbs and appears suddenly like them in breaking news. Massacre resembles my friends, but always arrives before them in faraway villages and children's schools.

Massacre is a dead metaphor that comes out of the television and eats my friends without a single pinch of salt.

—Ghayath Almadhoun, *Adrenalin*

A threshold is a sill, boundary, or limit point. It points to a within and a without, or at least to an either side of, a point beyond which something is true or a given effect is discernible or becomes intolerable, as in pain. Language is a kind of threshold. The two poems speak complexly to its doubleness: to its capacity to extend meaning and texture experience, and equally to its potential to deaden and distort it. And both can be—indeed, often are—simultaneously in play. Hence the irony, wit, and unsettling clarity of these poems. One cannot stand apart from them. We are thrust headfirst into the gravitational force of their epistemological challenge. The poems achieve something quite marvelous. They conjure a shared space in which, for example, the subject of the poem, the dedicated activist, the uninvolved reader, and the literary analyst can recognize themselves and simultaneously recognize each other *in* themselves.

These poems foreground the question of language. The disciplines that tend toward documenting—history, the social sciences, journalism—have dominated political and intellectual discourses in India and other parts of the global south. This fact has been a strength and a weakness. Politics is the imaginative discipline of living together artfully. And social movements ideally function as creative laboratories that incubate these futures. But for too long we have tended to practice politics as if it were primarily an agonistic battle between communities and those institutions that deny them their rights. Hard as this battle is proving to be, it pales in comparison with what it would require for us to unlearn and relearn in order to live together without prejudice, without recourse to law to ensure kindness and decency. For this deeper transformation, we need to rethink the way we have hitherto construed—or *failed* to construe—our interrelatedness, that which links, separates, and unites us: the dance of specificity, commonality, and difference within us and between us.

To relate is also to narrate. The question of language is thus inseparable from the fact of our mutuality—a mutuality we have resisted and distorted by means of a number of violent stratagems of othering, among them caste, gender, sexuality, race. To point to our intricate webbing with each other is not to deny the distortions of prevailing social norms. It is to recall the importance of continually marking the fictional nature of socially produced divisions such as caste or gender even as we map the devastating consequences of casteism and patriarchy. Caste is a myth but casteism is a reality; claims about gender inferiority are a fallacy but gender-based discrimination is real.

The vehement opposition and hostility that meet challenges to existing hierarchies have often led to a flattening of complexity, to a failure to distinguish sharply enough between the real effects of a fiction like race or caste supremacy and the nonreality of that fiction. As a result, our rhetoric can paradoxically reinscribe as real what we ourselves claim to be socially invented differences. The challenge of repairing what ideology has self-interestedly taken apart is in this process forfeited. Reductionism serves short-term polemics. But a sustained struggle for transformation depends on finding language that captures the full range of the specificities, similarities, commonalities, and differences that intersect to shape human experience.

Ghayath Almadhoun's poems present a profound challenge to the simplifying binaries that structure our thinking. They play with the absurdist and forked-tongue aspects of our deployment of language. They embed multiple subject positions in challenging us to rethink grief and massacre, turning both terms inside out on the page before us. Is grief an object, not just a subjective state? What does it mean to be able to purchase a grief and be happy with the choice? Why is the idea of existential angst as a form of self-fashioning uncannily familiar? Are Almadhoun's friends in Massacre its victims or its newly empowered progeny? Is it possible that they are both? What is the poet trying to say? Almadhoun's pieces unsettle because they estrange us from our assumptions. We are never quite sure of our footing. To engage his work is to be led to the broader question of the currents and crosshairs within which our understanding has come to be what it is. And relatedly to how we respond when the ground of meaning shifts beneath us. To read his words is to experience a kind of semiotic vertigo.

Political discourse would be revitalized by this kind of exuberant yet precise linguistic play. For despite obdurate evidence to the contrary, a reductive idea of absolute difference continues to haunt our rhetoric. We need language supple enough to accommodate difference as distinction, difference as specificity, difference as the effect of ideology, difference as a species of the diversity of nature, and difference as evidence of the varieties of human expression. The particularities of perception, identities, subject positions, experiences, senses of belonging and outsiderness are an effect of manifold forces and entanglements, each of which is itself multiply constituted. Our frameworks and discourses need to speak adequately to the heterogeneous and overlapping processes within which our lives take shape. Interdependence implies that all phenomena are relationally produced. We may seem to inhabit divergent cognitive worlds, but our lives are always entwined. The equitable remaking of already existing interdependencies is the only credible basis for imagining our future.

It no longer suffices only to marshal truths yet unspoken or document facts yet unacknowledged. Neoliberal capitalism has even more thoroughly hollowed out what it means to be human, making critical the integration into political praxis of broader questions about the meaning, purpose, and significance of human life and action. When connectivity and isolation have been heightened in equal measure, the potential for self-doubt is magnified and the sense of one's efficacy in the world correspondingly diminished. In this context the question of meaning becomes poignant—at times a matter of life and death. The prophetic and poetic dimension of language becomes crucial.

In its expansive sense politics is not a set of prescriptions for tactical moves against an external enemy, but a dynamic, open-ended personal and collective inquiry into human potential. We are far more than the categories that describe our social experience. And far more intimately interconnected with each other and the rest of the phenomenal world than recognized by the fissures and divides of prevailing frameworks. Politics can only renew itself if its discourse is open to incorporating these facts—not as slogans, but as its very raison d'être and promise.

eighteen ▼ continual evolution

our capacity to change depends
on our propensity to be altered
fragility a prerequisite for transformation

trees bend into the wind
oceans erode coastlines
seeds await gusts to be scattered
nature wears itself thin to the elements

evolution a continual remaking
nothing is stock-still, unmoving
even in death perpetual motion
a breaking down, a reabsorption

nineteen ▼ am i doing enough?

CRISIS, ACTIVISM, AND
THE SEARCH FOR MEANING

DURING THE EARLY MONTHS OF 2016, India's public universities were rocked by political turmoil. In a prefiguration of what was to become a defining feature of the rule of the right-wing Bharatiya Janata Party, the exercise of constitutionally guaranteed democratic rights began to be systematically criminalized. At Hyderabad Central University the institutional harassment of first-generation Dalit activists for organizing around social and political issues (suspension of stipends, ban on entry into university buildings, eviction from dorms) prompted Rohith Vemula to take his life in despair. In Jawaharlal Nehru University it led to the imprisonment of left-wing student leaders Kanhaiya Kumar, Umar Khalid, and Anirbhan Bhattacharya on charges of sedition. In both instances a witch hunt led by the media and the ruling party created a hostile environment not conducive to reason or a calm consideration of facts. The state had finally extended to university campuses ideological, legal, and political tactics long used against communities resisting development in rural India (Sainath 2016). To dissent was to be antinational, to nullify one's fundamental rights, to merit the full punitive force of state power. The unrest spread to other campuses and gripped the nation's attention.

During periods such as the one just described, we are usually observing the coming to fruition of social and political phenomena several decades in the making. Even so, one can subjectively experience the events as heralding a seismic atmospheric shift. It is hard to turn away from what feels like history unfolding in real time. But history only ever unfolds in real time. Indeed, history is the narrative seizure of a certain conception of time as real. Linear, measurable, objective: time summoned as im/partial witness. That said, there are periods when each moment, every twist and turn of the plot seems to thrum with significance. At such times we confront questions that are at the very heart of the human journey: How should I act? What should I do in these circumstances?

For those in the thick of unfolding events, pragmatic demands may dictate what must be done. For the arrested students—and their friends, families, lawyers, teachers, the communities of which they are a part—the answers may seem to be self-evident. Journalists and analysts who have been studying these events may also know what they must do in the short run. But what about those of us who are not close to the epicenter? What are we to do?

The sense of being witness to historic events may keep us glued to television and social media. Being informed is a form of responsible citizenship, especially when the battle being fought is explicitly ideological. Have you read, heard, seen? This news? Analysis? Speech? Cartoon? Photo? Meme? Post? Keeping track and sharing with others can feel like a form of civic participation. And to a degree it is. Beyond a point, however, it can feel insufficient. One might wish one were closer to the action, doing more. Self-doubt and self-judgment can arise in tandem and result in one spending more time online to compensate for the unease. The addictive potential of social media facilitates this mode of staving off a sense of inefficacy.

It may be tempting to conclude that the sense of insufficiency is an effect of distance, that those close to the events are spared this kind of doubt. But that is not necessarily true. Such moments pose existential questions: What is the meaning, purpose, and value of my actions and, by implication, my life? Should I be living it in some other way? What do my actions reveal about who I am? The answers to these difficult questions are individual-personal and collective-sociocultural. But to the degree that we are not aware of the pressure they may exert in us, we unconsciously seek to resolve their destabilizing effects through action that primarily assures *us* that we are doing *something*, that we are not simply mute spectators to a crisis. A sense of urgency cum insufficiency may prompt us to act in ways that contribute more heat than light, more noise than clarity.

chapter nineteen

Am I doing enough? The question haunts social justice activists, all who yearn to end needless suffering. It can lead to fatigue, indifference to self-care, rage at others for not doing enough, drugs and alcohol as a way to cope with the horror of injustice. Grief at the magnitude of problems to be addressed and frustration with our failure to resolve them can serve to create conditions in which divisiveness, othering, sectarianism, and disregard can emerge not just as legible reactions but as *credible* strategies for social transformation. We can forget that our politics anticipates our futures, that we, too, will reap what we sow.

To interpret the revolving door of rage, sorrow, despair, frustration, and hope as understandable responses to systemic injustice would be to miss something deeper. Heightened crisis brings into sharp relief a conundrum at the heart of our existence within a complexly interdependent social and natural world. The actualities of this world are at odds with three ideas that accrue particular poignancy during crisis periods and bear directly on the question of whether we are doing enough: our conception of action, significance, and impact. Our doubts about the efficacy and value of what we are doing or could be doing are partly a consequence of how we have come to think about these closely related terms.

Action-significance-impact. In our outward-oriented instrumentalist age, action must be seen to have extrinsic impact in order to be deemed significant. The effects of action on the world/on something other than the initiating subject should be nameable, traceable, in some way measurable even if not precisely quantifiable. This conception depends on a mechanistic and simplistic understanding of cause-and-effect interrelations. It cannot admit the mutability of subject-object boundaries, the difficulty of firmly separating the intrinsic from the extrinsic, and the enormous complexity of specifying, let alone grasping, the reality of near-infinite causes generating near-infinite effects. To acknowledge these facts is not to conclude that analysis is impossible but to point to its necessarily partial, situated, and open-ended character.

A mechanistic instrumentalism excludes much of what we as humans do. For instance, what could be more significant than breathing? Or more impactful on those connected to us and from whom the cessation of breath would separate us? Yet within this purview breath can never be deemed enough. One would strive to put it to "use," endow it with meaning and purpose to demonstrate we are indeed "alive" not "merely breathing." Even the deliberate termination of breath, as with Rohith Vemula's suicide, requires the redemption of a politics of action. Suicide-murder quickly morphs into sacrifice-martyrdom and seeks to be memorialized—in Vemula's case, by a law bearing his name that is intended to prevent others from being similarly cornered by institutional recalcitrance. The vividly resonant mind-heart-life immortalized in his parting letter makes way for a symbol, the particular for the abstract (Vemula 2016). Inevitable? Perhaps. But should we not draw breath to consider the irony that the campaign to support Dalit students in higher education repeats many of the same reductive gestures Rohith so movingly and critically called out in his suicide letter? Must something be made of his death for his life to have mattered? Was his life not intrinsically meaningful? Does it acquire significance only if History bears witness? Would it have amounted to nothing if his was one among the countless deaths that are privately, not publicly, mourned?

We may concede these points readily once they are plainly stated. But the gravitational pull of current political discourse draws us in a different direction: into a perspective in which action is most associated with activity undertaken on x in order to achieve y, with value and significance being aligned to the success of our endeavor. Meaning is rarely sought in the action itself. The link between significance and impact is thus continually cemented. To conceive of efficacy in these terms is to set oneself up to perennially wait for signs of success, to be acutely conscious of the work still to be done, vulnerable to feeling that one is not doing enough. It is not a sustainable orientation.

If our practices are to replenish and not deplete, we must rearticulate social justice discourse in an anticapitalist direction that affirms sentience and honors immanence. We must embrace meaning and value as a priori qualities inherent in all persons and things. People are more than the rights that accrue to them, and nonhuman nature is vibrantly alive and greater than its utility to humans. Value, meaning, and significance must be decoupled from effect, consequence, impact, and success. Meaning and significance are intrinsic to action regardless of whether the prevailing framework considers a given activity or gesture to be inconsequential. Our activism does not ensure value (either ours or that of the issue at hand) but simply reaffirms it in context of challenging socially produced miasmas and hierarchies. To reorient ourselves in this way is to open to an ethic of action free of the anxiety of efficacy, an anxiety that has led us to search for meaning everywhere but where it actually resides: In every breath. In all things. In all that we are. In all that we do.

twenty ▼ the tantra of action

"WHAT SHOULD I DO?" This question is one that many of us probably ask ourselves with some degree of regularity. At times it may arise in the context of self-doubt or self-judgment. More often, however, the question expresses concern about how to meet what life has deposited at our door. During times of intensive collective experiences such as a pandemic, war, or social unrest, the question assumes a particular poignancy. Even as we may wish to do something useful, the sheer scale of the crisis or the require-ment—as with COVID-19—that we shelter in place may converge to make all but first responders feel helpless to do much at all.

But the question "What should I do?" is not as simple as the words might suggest. The word *doing* is freighted with conditioning. Not every-thing that would count as action would count as doing. The questions being asked of oneself are, "How may I be useful?" "What can I contribute?" And perhaps equally, "Can I feel my worth if I am unable to do what I think is valuable?" Maybe even, "Can I feel my worth if I am not *seen* to be doing what I think is useful?" We begin to recognize that the question of what to do quickly exceeds the current circumstance. It is one at the very heart of a human grappling with the meaning and significance of one's life.

The simplistic understanding of causation implicit in this intensely moral question of appropriate action does not help matters. It is a version of "cue hits billiard ball causing it to be pocketed." Effort–action–evidence of success in the realization of intent: the complexity of the real world rarely conforms to this idealized scenario. The result can be the experience of perpetual if low-grade self-doubt at the individual level. Even when a structural understanding is available of the broader context for the absence of success, the mediation is left to the individual to undertake, and the terms of analysis can remain unquestioned.

Tantra offers an understanding of cause and effect that is more appropriate to the facts of interdependence. Each aspect of life is seen to express a multiplicity of interrelationships, and each is seen as the conditioned or contingent effect of such interrelations. Everything—be it process or object, human or natural—is seen to manifest the principle of "this is like this because that is like that," what Buddhism describes as dependent co-arising. Everything is a dependent effect of a dependent cause, and each cause and every effect generates still other causes and effects in a near-infinite unfolding of processes. We are called on to set aside the sufficiency of a single or dominant cause, an approach that erects boundaries around processes that are uncontainable. Law, for the most part, still depends on an overly simplistic conception of sufficient cause and evidence, which is why environmental cases, for example, are so hard to prosecute.

The theoretical language may be unfamiliar to some, but the key point can be stated simply: we are an infinitesimal part of a complex whole in which everything that exists continually shapes, and is in turn shaped by, everything else. Our lives are lived along multiple timelines: geological, seasonal, political, ritual, historical, biorhythmic, cultural, cellular, cosmic, and so on. This is life in interdependence. We are not isolates subsisting in a nowhere but situated in space-time, an essential aspect *of*/essential actors *in* life's ebb and flow. And our perception and understanding are related to the *where* of our locatedness. It is from t/here that we each make sense of a world in continual motion. Naturally we can grasp only some aspects of it. Tantra honors this fundamental truth by inviting its practitioners to live in "don't know" and in recognition of their situatedness.

The idea that knowledge is situated has been a critical insight in feminist, race, queer, and postcolonial theory. But where in those debates there has been at times a tendency to imply (at times, to argue) that the most disadvantaged locations offer the clearest view of the whole, in tantra the principle of situatedness and the corollary of partial knowing is a priori without exception. Even my knowledge of my own location is necessarily partial. Grasping the truth of these twin insights inspires care and modesty in how one relates to the world. We are inclined toward cultivating curiosity as an orientation to life, opened to being transformed by what we encounter. In a time when the exaggerated sense of self-importance of one *sub*division of nature—humanity—has led to the extinction of so much planetary life, it is salutary to be reminded of the limits that are intrinsic to the very conditions of existence, to be relieved of the miasma of mastery.

Living in "don't know" and living in recognition of our situatedness constitute two of the five premises of a tantric orientation. The third is learning to set aside our preferences and deconditioning our ways of seeing; the fourth, taking joy in the process; and the last, trusting Spirit, the Divine, the laws of nature to shelter us on our journey. As we practice within this matrix we begin to gradually discover our purpose, our respons*ibility*, what we have come to do. And we set about the task of cultivating the requisite response *abilities*. Like any genuine path of inquiry, tantra does not offer a formula to be applied mechanically but a framework for understanding and a set of practices through which practitioners can validate its insights in light of their own experience.

The five orienting points of the tantric path are akin to lenses, each of which offers a distinct view. Each implies its own journey and involves wrestling with our conditioning. For example, if we ask what we should do in the context of setting aside preferences, we immediately confront our investments and attachments, the values we assign to various kinds of action. If we turn then to our location we begin to understand some of how and why we have come to think or feel as we do. Even as we produce an inventory for ourselves, however, we are aware that we cannot know *all* there is to know. The idea of the divine or of nature being in charge may bring relief from the ensuing uncertainty—or at least assure us that there will be support to enhance our capacity to meet prospective challenges with grace and grit. Alternately, one may feel irritation, even anger, at the discovery of limits to one's desire for knowledge and self-reliance. Relationality can begin to feel like a cruel constraint. We come face to face once more with our preferences. A dynamic of expansion and contraction, apparent gains and losses, characterizes the journey. Joy in the process alternates between being an effortless outcropping of mindful action and a promise withheld, an immaterial abstraction.

One of the challenges in asking the question, "What should I do?" in the present is that the dominant understanding of value is closely tied to the logic of utility, to what the market deems productive. Anything that falls outside the scope of this narrow conception, including work critical to reproducing everyday life—childcare, domestic work, care for the ill, for the elderly—is deemed less valuable and thus is poorly compensated. By extension, anyone deemed to be living an unproductive life in these terms carries the stigma of worthlessness. This view effectively excludes most humans and most of what life actually involves.

In tantra value is intrinsic. The tantric path celebrates the isness of all that exists, that is to say, its specific vibration and vibrancy. The practitioner leans into and learns from the isness of each thing, being, and activity. Fulfilment is in the doing, not in its consequence, impact, or social value. We understand cause and effect to be complex and learn to refrain from making quick judgments about importance and significance. To open to interdependence is to grasp the profound truth that no action is too small to be inconsequential. The effect of a butterfly flapping its wings in Tokyo can be a tornado in Mexico City. The deepening awareness of the complexly reciprocal nature of existence inspires modesty, enchants life, and enables joy in the process.

To know oneself to be part of nature is to surrender to it. Nature is continually evolving in the direction of a dynamic rebalancing and new equilibrium. Rebalancing is not always benign. Such transformations are processes of simultaneous creation/destruction, death/regeneration. We understand nature not to protect ourselves from it so much as to discern what it means to live in alignment with it. Free will may enable humans to resist respecting nature's laws, but they are applicable to us nonetheless, as many realize with dismay.

Tantra celebrates the very opposite of the predatory logic that has brought us the multiple crises—ecological, social, economic—we face today. The current order is based on a defiance of nature and life and can offer futures that are only variations of the dystopias we are already witnessing. Tantra, like other matter-loving, sentience-affirming wisdoms, offers a way forward that is grounded in alignment, not resistance; abundance, not scarcity; mutuality, not antagonism; subtlety, not simplification. It is a profound challenge to the ways of knowing and being that dominate today.

twenty-one ▼ "we inter are"

IDENTITY POLITICS AND #METOO[1]

CIRCA 1980S, USA

The politics of location
Theory in the flesh
The privilege of partial perspective
Oppositional consciousness

El Mundo Zurdo
Cables, esoesses
Conjurations & fusil missiles
Make (r)evolution irresistible

Polyvocal multilingual
Poetry prose polemic fiction
Displace reframe and recompose
The single as the multiverse

Even then Bambara warned
that wholeness was no trifling matter
"Are you sure, sweetheart?" she said
"A lot of weight when you're well"

This not-quite-poem is a bricolage of citations. Barring stanza three, it is composed almost entirely of the words of US feminists: Adrienne Rich (1986), Cherríe Moraga and Gloria Anzaldúa (1981), Donna Haraway (1988), Chela Sandoval (1991), Toni Cade Bambara (1980, 1981). The ideas they express emerge from, and intervene in, several interrelated histories—colonial, racial, ethnic, class, gendered, sexual, bodily. To follow their logic is to parse dominant ideas into ensembles of contingent facts.

The challenge to the so-called universal held a dual promise: a decolonization of mind and a reimagination of freedom. The insistent eruption of the diversity of experiences, perspectives, myths, metaphors, visions was never an end in itself (though the market did strive where it could to domesticate it as a species of variety). It was above all an interpretive summons: a call to rethink and re-vision pastspresentsfutures. To reexamine experience, to *specify* it. The call to arms was a call for complexity. Specification as a first step toward rethinking the interrelations that constitute the social-ecological whole.

The forms of expression reflected this impulse. Testimonials. Fiction. Historical excavation. Memoir. Oral history. Poetry. Ceremonies. Fantasy. Biomythography. Theory. The *inter* of relations refracted in the imploding of timelines, concepts, and domains, in the trans-creation of literary genres, the visual arts, and theater. The material-nonmaterial, analytical-spectral, psychic-spiritual, ideological-poetic combining in new ways to speak—*to, from, for, with, of, near*—beauty, desire, justice, history, law, and love. Binaries were inverted, subverted, on occasion subtended. In the exuberance of the moment, structure/subject, individual/community, history/agency, nature/culture, body/mind, subject/object all appeared poised to slough off the weight of history and point to terra incognita.

▼

The subsequent trajectory of this flourishing is disparaged as "identity politics." On the Right it is dismissed as hateful and socially divisive. Many liberals feel it has gone too far in disrupting a shared social compact. On the Left there is concern that identity has usurped class.

Black Lives Matter and the Water Protectors at Standing Rock (contemporary US movements that provoke the greatest ire) give lie to claims of divisiveness and of indifference to collective well-being. Both offer a profound critique of US economy and culture, its fossil-fueled racist necropolitics, its commitment to little more than bare life for those within and outside its borders. Both re-vision society in ways expansive and inclusive. Both exemplify moral courage, political acuity, nonviolence. The transformations they seek are not narrowly racial or nationalist but collective and transnational, spiritual as well as political. They ask us to attend with care to the inter-webbing of life. Like their forbears, they unravel the false binaries that continue to structure our thinking.

Identity politics has encountered the same hostility that has historically met movements for redressal of injustice. Every life-affirming principle that grounds its redreaming of society is caricatured by those in power. Inclusion of the hitherto excluded is deemed exclusion of the hitherto included. Justice for all is considered injustice for the privileged. Pluralizing ideas to account for a diversity of experience is regarded as a dilution of excellence. It would seem, as George Orwell (1949) says in *1984*, "War is peace. Freedom is slavery. Ignorance is strength."

To argue that one's location in the social structure shapes one's perception and experience is not to suggest that this relationship is self-evident. The question of how it should be understood is a matter of intense debate, not just across positionings in the social structure (gender, race, class, or sexuality, in India caste) but within them also. These matters can never fully be settled, making feminism (like other movements) an always evolving, argumentative sphere.

Form and genre are at the heart of such creative contention. The relations between location and knowledge are proffered in multiple, overlapping ways. Asserted via polemic. Demonstrated by means of argument. Gradually unfolded in a novel, anthology, film, or play. Obliquely or directly invoked in a poem, song, or rap. Transformed ritually by ceremony and storytelling. Reimagined in speculative fantasy. Defamiliarized by satire, wit. Conjured by visuality's lucid dreaming and startling clarity. Each form is a specific invitation to seeing, feeling, and knowing anew. A doorway to terra currently incognita. Each addresses the interrelations between being and knowing, the particular and the whole, in the register most appropriate to it.

Forms and genres carry specific burdens. The expressive arts, fiction, poetry enable us to experience the skin, soul, and energy of ideas. They may delineate certain connections, merely hint at others. The more didactic forms—argument, assertion, analysis—are obliged to explicate. In them it very much matters how a problem is framed, what connections are made, what is deemed significant and what not. One does not wish to overstate the difference. Both make sense of experience. Through the expressive arts we *sense the making* of experience, its coming into being. The didactic arts help us *make sense* of experience, render it intelligible. The processes are distinct but not firmly separable.

▼

Specificity as a first step toward rethinking interrelations: the potential of identity politics is most fully realized when this insight is properly integrated. And it is here that even those who practice it may fall short. As an example, I draw on the debate around #MeToo. Sex, sexual pleasure, sexual liberation, sexual harassment, and sexual violence have always been central feminist concerns. But the current explosion of testimony about harassment and assault is arguably without parallel. Across the globe, women from every sector of society have spoken out. Some have named their abusers. Others have chosen not to. In India, a list that anonymously accused a number of male academics of harassment was shared widely on the internet. #MeToo has also included men attesting to harassment, naming male and, in a couple of instances, female harassers. Unsurprisingly, most stories have been have been about male assaults on women.

Sexual abuse may be described as a violation of interrelatedness. A distortion and negation of the mutuality that is existence. Even as we are inescapably individual, and distinguishable as such, we exist in always already prevailing relations of intimacy—I would go so far as to say, of intersubjectivity. This is probably why the violation of one's will or body is so thoroughly dispiriting. Something elemental is dishonored. I do not locate sexual violence outside of history or culture, for it is an indisputably *social* phenomenon. But interrelatedness as a priori might explain some of the affective intensity around the issue; why hostility haunts disagreements in ways that exceed what is attributable to a polarized climate and social media norms.

There has been a generational aspect to the differences. In the US, this has been the most evident in relation to author Junot Díaz (whose revelation of childhood sexual abuse was followed by women testifying to his subsequent abuse of them during his adulthood)[2] and philosopher Avital Ronell (accused of sexual abuse by a male graduate student).[3] In India the generational difference was most evident in relation to the list of male academics named as harassers.[4] At times it has seemed as though the pain and anguish of younger feminists has been inaudible to older feminists, its viscerality eclipsed by, or subordinated to, specific concerns. In the US, this has included fear among some of a rerun of the sex wars of the 1980s, a bolstering of a puritanical cultural seam, concerns with due process and Title IX, trial by social media, and, in the Díaz case, racial dynamics. Not everyone has shared all of these concerns. In India, the disagreement has devolved primarily around the absence of due process in the circulation of a list of male names without details of accusations or accusers; not far behind, however, has followed the same worry about creeping moralism in the context of the ruling party's social conservatism.

A significant shift in context partly accounts for some of the difference in perspective. In the US, the sexual freedoms fought for by the generation that came of age during the 1960s are taken for granted by those currently in their twenties or thirties. They require no "defense." A diverse sexual landscape characterizes the present with a wide range of gender and sexual self-naming. At the same time, the pressure to be sexually active (compulsory sexuality?) seems to have produced its own counterreaction, with some young people consciously choosing celibacy and asexuality. Economic precarity has also widened the generational gulf. The neoliberal capture of the academy and the uncertain future facing graduate students has shaped the US conversation about pedagogy, power, fear, and the star system in the Avital Ronell case.

Specific to India, the expansion of higher education has opened universities to first-generation students. Many have felt pressured by the equation of modernity and freedom with a certain form of sexual self-expression. Uncomfortable but unable to stand their ground, when the opportunity to tell their stories and name names presented itself, the arguments for due process felt like one more admonition. Given the pervasive nature of sexual harassment and the abysmal record of legal and institutional redress, the cumulative power of a collective naming of abuse (and at times of an abuser) took precedence over all other considerations.

A vital debate has ensued and excellent analysis has been produced. But fault lines quickly emerged, transforming the noisy public square into a nasty one. Disagreements about how sexual assault should be understood and addressed have been attributed to race, status, age, caste—sometimes justifiably, sometimes not. Each side has accused the other of failing to understand the negative consequences of positions taken. Concerns about "trigger culture" and the neoliberal production of brittle subjects have not been equally shared. There has been much talking past each other, much intemperate discourse. It is not hard to see why things unfolded in this way. And yet, it was not inevitable. Feminist insight regarding specificity and interrelations could have enabled a thinking *with* the multidimensionality being expressed.

Why has it been difficult to get analytical hold of the emerging discourse beyond binary descriptions such as pro or anti due process; pro or anti Ronell; or as a standoff between sex radicals and sex moralists? How does one account for the absence of an appropriate engagement with relevant facts of abuse/abusive subcultures in interventions authors would deem "principled"? What is lost if the present is seen via the lens of past feminist divides? Why does calling out abuse negate eros; is the line between them really that indistinguishable? Does one abuse elide another or in any way explain it?

The problem is partly one of genre. Much of the discussion has unfolded through dispersed serial interventions via forms that require brevity and privilege opinion, reportage, and rebuttal. It is up to readers to synthesize the different threads of conversation. However, the volume of expression and the fleeting nature of these media make such synthesis difficult. The destructive effects and diminishing returns of discursive shredding are all too evident. Social media posts, blogs, news articles, and op-eds cannot stage layered, intertextual, cumulative encounters with culture, power, narrative frames, pain, skin, and soul. We need forms that facilitate prismatic explorations of the themes that have emerged.

Perhaps #MeToo can become raw material for more textured (re)considerations of issues, an archive for art and other interventions. For example, a reader of discussions around Junot Díaz could gather his heart-wrenching account of sexual abuse during early childhood, the equally moving narratives of many he later treated carelessly or abused, the open letter from feminists alerting us to the racial politics of reception in this case, the interventions of scholars in Puerto Rican Studies. And alongside, a call for fresh submissions and the opportunity to rewrite/overwrite/ghostwrite. Such a collection would offer a for(u)m capacious enough to think with and through the intersectional and interstitial of experience, the true promise of identity politics.

NOTES

1 I borrow "We Inter Are" from Thich Nhat Hahn's poem "Interrelationship" (1999).

2 The discussions around Dominican American author Junot Díaz were sparked by a searing article he published in 2018 in the *New Yorker* detailing the continuing impact on him of child sexual abuse. Although in that essay Díaz admits the negative consequences of the abuse for his adult relationships with women, the piece galvanized a number of women writers—among them Zinzi Clemmons, Carmen Maria Machado, Monica Byrne, and Shreerekha—to detail Díaz's sexual misconduct and verbal abuse toward them (Alter, Bromwich, and Cave 2018; Shreerekha 2018). Also reprised was the question of the misogyny in Díaz's representation of women, leading to the wide circulation of the poem "How to Know You Are a Woman in a Junot Díaz Novel" (Rodriguez 2017). As coverage of Díaz grew, concerns about racism as a dynamic of reporting led a number of feminist scholars to publish an open letter in the *Chronicle of Higher Education* (de Jesús et al. 2018), prompting a rebuttal from other largely younger feminists of color who argued the priority of survivor support (Ahluwalia et al. 2018) and a clarification and defense of the original letter by Linda Alcoff, one of its signatories (Alcoff 2018; Flaherty 2018).

3 Avital Ronell, a queer philosopher on the faculty at NYU, was accused of sexual harassment by her former gay doctoral student, Nimrod Reitman. An internal investigation found Reitman's accusations to be credible, and Ronell was sent on a year's leave without pay, but not before a who's who of feminist and other poststructuralist theorists rose to her defense even without access to the full details of the matter (Leiter 2018). The Ronell case has raised a panoply of issues from pedagogy and power to the changed economic and institutional context of graduate education (Chu 2018; Duggan 2018; Gessen 2018; Robin 2018; Robinson 2018).

4 In India, discussions ignited by #MeToo flared up in context of Raya Sarkar's crowdsourced list of male academics accused of sexually harassing their students. The list, which did not name accusers nor detail accusations, signaled both an unaddressed crisis in academic life and despair over the insufficiency of available institutional redress (Shankar 2017; Tiwary and Sriraman 2017). Its publication sparked furious debate around due process, which broadly appeared to reveal a generational and, some argued, caste divide (Krishnan 2017; Menon 2017; Online Desk 2017; Rowena 2017; Sunitha et al. 2017).

twenty-two ▼ a malleable border
teeming with life

ONE OF THE MOST DIFFICULT ASPECTS of the COVID-19 pandemic has been the specter of tens of thousands dying without the solace of being surrounded by loved ones. Of poignant images of faces and palms pressed against the windows of nursing homes in the US and elsewhere. Of goodbyes over phone calls and FaceTime. Of scattered kin keeping vigil in far-flung places without each other for comfort. These stories snagged the heart and tripped the mind as we struggled to imagine lives slipping away in the cold sterility of a hospital setting.

Yet many who work with the dying know that the transition we call death is a malleable border teeming with life. It is rarely spoken of publicly. Death may be universal, but each passing feels intensely private. It belongs to those closest to the person who has departed. Every detail of those last weeks, days, hours—the decisions, confusions, tensions, emotions, even the very atmosphere—is saturated with meaning. The time constitutes our final experience of a person, and our memories assume a resonant quality. Families may diverge in their responses and recollections. But it is rare that anyone close to the event is left untouched. Death pries open the heart in a very particular way. One is acutely aware of having been witness to an elemental event. And it can be unnerving to risk others' incomprehension of, or embarrassment at, the intensity of our feelings. Consequently, although it was precisely death's universality that made it a primordial experience, it can retreat once again into the realm of the private.

Not so for those who have worked with the dying. To us the dialectic of the individual and the universal in death is an evident truth regularly witnessed. Death may be social, but it is also nature expressing itself. Those who provide end-of-life care witness its rhythms and its unspoken dimensions. In the context of a pandemic that has isolated death inside institutions and shattered even the possibility of a partially shared process, it seems important to speak to some of what is rarely named, in case doing so brings comfort to the bereaved. What I say will not be news to many in palliative care or living/dying movements across the world. Others may consider it to be patently absurd. Such readers are invited to contemplate what follows as a thought experiment.

No one dies alone. Everyone is helped with their transition. Those who know they are terminally ill may prepare themselves. But they, too, are accompanied. Dying is not a singular event but a process. As this process unfolds, the dying person's consciousness gradually begins to expand beyond the frames of human cognition. The subjective experience of time slows down so as to facilitate it. The pace is determined by an individual's willingness and readiness. If necessary, the integration of the transition may continue after it has occurred. Such is the compassion of the universe.

Where the death is sudden and unexpected, the process may even be initiated after the person has crossed over. Those assisting are spirit kin whom the individual recognizes as consciousness expands beyond the human. No one is coerced. Although from a human perspective the earthly self may not have "chosen" the death, its broader context is grasped once the transition occurs. This is not to suggest that all deaths are just. Humans are endowed with free will, a capacity that, as we know, is used to heal as well as to harm, to create as well as to destroy. Deaths can be unwarranted and untimely, the consequence of neglect, violence, injustice. Mourning such needless deaths is not just a transpersonal but a crossborder phenomenon. Violation is violation regardless of the realm.

What I state here challenges religious belief and rationality as currently conceived. I cannot and will not aim to convince. Is assertion, then, all I can offer? Yes and no. Death is commonly thought to be scary. But many who have been close to it have also been privy to the atmosphere of peace that can prevail around the person in their last days and hours. In an inversion of expectations, the energy in a patient's room can contrast sharply with the tumult in the waiting room, where death as idea prevails over dying as process. The rise and fall of shallow breaths, the beeping of monitors, the unconscious person, physically restless, gasping for breath, crying out in pain: life pared to bare essentials brings one sharply into the present. The dying person and the one keeping vigil are in the same temporal zone. The quality of silence amid the uncertainty and grief can be palpable, supportive, hard to fathom.

If death led only to the silence of the grave, we would be hard put to explain visitations from the dead to those left behind, experiences that usually bring assurance and comfort to the living. One has not heard of husbands returning to finish a quarrel or of creditors threatening debtors over money owed. Further, those who have returned to life after near-death experiences have spoken in remarkably consistent ways about having been enveloped in indescribable love and of having encountered beings who strive to guide humans but can do so only if we cooperate (Alexander 2012; Eadie 1992). Then there are mediums who bring messages from the beyond by request. Those who communicate even while sounding like their earthly selves may speak with greater wisdom than they evinced when they were in a body, suggesting that their human incarnation was only a partial iteration of who they are.

These are not arguments. They are at best partial clues. Perhaps my perspective will speak only to those who are already inclined to find it intelligible. But if these words serve to ease even a little bit of the pain over a family member or friend having died alone, the risk of sharing will be worthwhile. And given the scale of the number of deaths from COVID-19, I will settle for a sliver of curiosity about what I have described. For it may prompt reflection on energies or presences that might have been sensed but dismissed as improbable, or inexplicable moments when acceptance of the situation became possible and calm descended, even if temporarily. The knowledge that beings are supported on the other side may also serve to soothe the pain of deaths in which much remains unresolved. It may lead some to undertake rituals of mourning with a little more trust that those who have departed may also be renewed by the celebration of their lives.

Many boundaries have been pushed and redrawn in order to enable a fuller accounting of the human experience. That supposedly separating life and death, the human and spirit realms, has not been one of them. Could it be an idea whose time has come?

afterword

MYRIAD INTIMACIES has sought to enact a mode of thinking about inter-relations. Of lives, concepts, aspects of self. Of spirit, matter, humanity's relationship with the rest of nature. Its explorations—fragmentary, tentative, assertive, argumentative—have moved between text and image. A shared set of concerns have been examined in some of their variations. Each time from a different angle, with a different inflection, in a different form or domain. If this attempt has succeeded even to a small degree, you will have noted, and in some cases perhaps experienced, the play of specificity, diversity, and relatedness, the multiplicity of time.

A recursive dynamic characterizes the collection and is a convergence of several factors. Many of the subjects that impel this inquiry—desire, identity, poetics, body, rhetoric, love, the sacred—are intrinsically exploratory. This is equally true of the tantric premises that are a root inspiration: relationality as constitutive of existence, matter as sentient, thought as sensuous activity, the sensual as cognitive capacity. One cannot merely seize such ideas and make them one's own. One lives with, ponders, and gradually allows oneself to learn from the dance of cogitation and revelation. Their force is most keenly felt when they come alive as experience, when a proposition is made flesh. It is an incremental and iterative process. To be authentic to it calls for an approach that is an invitation to reflect rather than an exhortation to agree. It integrally raises questions of form and genre. And it embraces its locatedness in space-time.

As I prepared to submit *Myriad Intimacies* for review in late spring 2020, my Oakland neighborhood erupted, along with the rest of the nation, in grief and righteous rage over the murder of George Floyd by the Minneapolis police on May 25. The violence was undertaken casually before members of the public, one of whom recorded the traumatic incident on her cell phone. Pinned to the ground with a policeman's knee pressing down on his neck, Floyd could be heard desperately pleading that he could not breathe until his body goes limp. It was shattering to watch the footage. The indifference of police toward Floyd and the lack of concern at their actions being filmed by a public seeking to intervene on his behalf provoked unprecedented national and global outcry. The moment dramatized the continued legacy of colonization, slavery, and racism more so since it came during a viral pandemic known to have disproportionately affected African Americans, Latinos, and Native Americans. The charge of brutality as endemic to policing was further confirmed by police violence against the predominantly peaceful multiracial protests that swept the country in response.

Some curfews were lifted. Some Confederate statues were dismantled. Promises were made that some police budgets would be slashed and reallocated for community health and development. The term *systemic racism* began to circulate in public discussion. The US Navy and Marines moved to ban the Confederate flag, and the Army declared its intention to follow suit. The beginning of summer 2020 seemed to herald a renewed phase in the struggle to deepen civil rights and ensure racial justice in the United States. The pushback, however, or more accurately, retribution, came swiftly enough. An intense battle unfolded over what it meant to reckon with the continuing impact and myriad afterlives of colonization, slavery, and white supremacy. Matters were made more incendiary with President Trump openly inciting violence against those calling for a reckoning with history and urging far-right fascist groups to take matters into their own hands. Predominantly peaceful protestors met with a militarized response and were reviled as hateful looters while right-wing militia were dubbed patriots and extended the full protection of law. Trump also used his executive power as a punitive weapon, issuing on September 4, 2020, an order that declared diversity, inclusion, and equity work as divisive, un-American propaganda and withholding federal funding from any institution that undertook it. The air was dense with outright lies and obfuscations. All this even as the pandemic intensified hunger, illness, and unemployment. Meanwhile, not only was there no official plan to respond to the pandemic, but the veracity of the virus continued to be challenged and mask mandates and other public health initiatives actively undermined. Cruelty and callousness were ubiquitous, relentless, unbearable. It felt surreal.

▼

In meditative practice we turn to breath to gain some distance from the restlessness of mind. As we direct our awareness to the breath entering our nostrils and descending to our bellies, we fall beneath the tumult of mental activity in which we may have been entangled and become aware of all that it might have served to obscure. A process somewhat akin to this one was observable in the din that characterized the public sphere in the summer and autumn of 2020. Notwithstanding the Trump administration's efforts to volubly distract, divert, deny, and divide, the primacy of breath was asserting itself everywhere and at every turn. This elemental sign of life became a subject of daily, near continual discussion: In the fact that COVID-19 was airborne and required our commitment to physically distance from one another. In how the virus attacked the respiratory tract, requiring us to wear masks. In the absence of sufficient ventilators or hospital staff trained to use them. In the death by asphyxiation of Eric Garner and George Floyd (Mbembe 2020; Perry 2019). In the emergence of "I Can't Breathe" as a potent slogan and rallying cry during demonstrations against police violence. In the Movement for Black Lives naming as "The Breathe Act" its draft legislation for reimagining policing. In the warnings about the concentration of carbon in the atmosphere and the looming threat of climate catastrophe. In the relation between pollution and compromised immune function that made poor populations especially vulnerable to COVID-19.

Even as an officially sanctioned corrosive divisiveness seemed to dominate, it was being revealed as a miasma. We were being constantly reminded that that which sustains life is impervious to being divided, segregated, or contained. That breath connects us. That one individual's inhalation is inseparable from another's exhalation. That although air quality varied widely, neither air nor any of the elements could be sequestered. That things we insist on seeing as unconnected are intricately interwoven. Even while our minds and hearts may have been preoccupied with battling the fatigue of being bombarded with lies and distortions, core principles of nature were being repeatedly brought to our attention and enacted in innumerable mutual aid efforts and practices of care that blossomed within social movements and community projects. Signs big and small of creative collaboration, cooperation, concern for others. However, it took a Herculean effort of will to simultaneously hold in one's consciousness both the destructive and the generative dynamics of this period. For one effect of the tendency toward androcentrism and the primacy it accords to human agency and realpolitik is that we are more likely to be caught up with—and persuaded by—power's commitment to extinguishing radical hope than the revolutionary potential of the concerted efforts of some humans to align with nature's "tendential lines of force" (Hall 1996, 42). Horrified by the violence of power's mendacity, we can fail to sufficiently notice, draw succor from, and integrate countless mutinies, spectacular as well as quotidian, and mounting evidence that the modes of extraction underwriting forms of life currently deemed desirable are already unsustainable relics, dystopic nonfutures.

▼

At the heart of political and cultural conflicts today is a struggle over whether to respect the elegant diversity and nonarbitrary coherence of life on this planet. We are an exquisitely diverse inextricable whole. Out of the one, many. In the one, every. Those who deny this truth effectively sign a pact with fear, suspicion, hostility, hatred, and violence. They remain wedded to the very ideas that have brought us the current crisis, social as well as environmental. Their truculence renders them uniquely incapable of thinking. Their answer to the call to recognize facts and reimagine the future seems always to be a resounding NO! Their policies prescribe, proscribe, discipline, displace, control, punish, eliminate. Their discourse is repetitive, monotonous, tedious. It moves in a shrinking direction, doubling in on itself and doubling down on its assumptions. If it manifests any vigor at all, it is usually an effect of its malevolence. The sting, though enervating, is transitory and requires resuscitation by further egregiousness in word and deed. From a tantric standpoint this tendency toward tedium and the need for continual reiteration are consequences of such discourses not being congruent with the principles of nature. The institutions of global capitalism and the governments beholden to them belong here, as do ideologues on the Right who are committed to a politics of malice.

In stark contrast, those who are open to the vibrancy and integrity of each entity and every mode of existence innovate imaginatively, expansively, inclusively. Their alignment with nature's exuberant diversity unleashes boundless creativity. They contribute a seemingly endless stream of ideas and blueprints for addressing the many aspects of human and nonhuman life currently under duress. Their solutions are not narrowly sectarian but include as needed reform, revolution, restitution, restoration, revival, redressal, and reparations. And alongside, reuse, recycling, and repair as simple antidotes to the planned obsolescence and wasteful consumption mandated by the market. They seed new articulations of politics, spirituality, nature, culture, mind, body, and the intellectual, creative, and healing arts. Movements across the globe to steward the environment and heal societal divisions of race, caste, gender, sexuality are examples. Many are led by youth, women, transpersons, and, importantly, indigenous peoples who have never forgotten first principles. They manifest enthusiasm, energy, an irresistible vitality. They inspire.

We return once again to breath.

Two slogans, "Black Lives Matter" and "Respect Existence or Expect Resistance," capture this well. Both are popular and express the spirit of this time. Both assert truths. Neither is a demand. Both, for different reasons, may be said to be akin to koans. Black Lives Matter. A succinct expression of what should not need to be stated but needs to be said again and again given slavery, Jim Crow, and the prison-industrial complex. To those who are aware of and disturbed by the history of racism, Black Lives Matter is a powerfully moving affirmation. Initially a hashtag to Alicia Garza's 2013 Facebook post "A Love Note to Black People," in which Garza protested George Zimmerman's acquittal in the February 26, 2012, murder of Trayvon Martin, it has since evolved into a mobilizing slogan and organizing idea for a broad social justice movement to protect and honor Black lives. Tens of thousands of every race and creed have joined with African Americans across the United States and around the world in attesting to its truth by emblazoning it on placards, T-shirts, posters, and other media. Those indifferent to white supremacy, however, or else explicitly committed to it, respond to Black Lives Matter as though it were a bewildering riddle that defies logic. "Don't all lives matter?" they ask petulantly. The question is not innocent. The slogan does not in any way imply that other lives do not matter. The response seeks to recast an affirmation of specificity as a claim of exclusivity and is itself a sign of the importance of asserting the sanctity of Black life.

Broad in scope, the slogan Respect Existence or Expect Resistance seems omnipresent in this time: in the campaign to raise the minimum wage to $15 an hour in the United States, as the title of a 2013 song by the Brazilian metal band Violator, at the historic Women's March on Washington against Trump in January 2017, at protests at the US-Mexico border, and against detention centers. On T-shirts, posters, mugs. As a meme on Instagram. And across the world in India it has been scrawled with chalk onto roads, stairwells, and walls in protests against the 2019 Citizenship Amendment Act, a law that explicitly discriminates against Muslims (Slater 2019). Unsurprisingly, it was the subject of one of the murals in downtown Oakland, where shopfronts that had been boarded up in the context of the protests against the murder of George Floyd and remaining shuttered because of the pandemic became canvases for a remarkable people's art project.

Respect Existence or Expect Resistance: the slogan gives pause. Who is it addressing? Certainly, the state and the institutional powers that be. "Look at me and take me into account," it seems to say, "or else you can expect me to assert my presence!" It is a summons to respect; it challenges the idea of disposability. But *existence* is an expansive term. It conjures more than individual, community, or nation. It encompasses everything that is alive. In a time when the environmental precipice at which the world is poised is a felt reality and not merely an idea, the slogan quickly expands to include each of us and all that exists. It turns out to be a truth that requires further reflection in order to be fully grasped. The longer one contemplates it the more there seems to be to it. Like a Ghayath Almadhoun poem, it embeds multiple subject positions.

We are all being addressed. But by whom? The words, to be sure. But the words call attention to a foundational principle: respect the nature of all that is alive or else you will surely experience a countervailing force. It could be Nature speaking to us. Gently alerting us to what we might expect if we are indifferent to her implicate order. Although if Nature were the author, perhaps *consequence* might have replaced *resistance*. For Nature does not "resist." It responds in accordance with its laws. The slogan speaks of the disruption that ensues when something essential about the nature of existence is not honored.

It is often said that slogans speak truth to power. But Black Lives Matter and Respect Existence or Expect Resistance go further. The first honors specificity and does so relationally. To claim Black Lives Matter is already to recognize other lives, to imagine that these interrelationships could be lived free of the detritus of history and injustice. The idea of an interdependent diversity is crucial to the movement's intersectional conception of politics, to its roots in women-of-color feminism and queer politics. Respect Existence or Expect Resistance also brings our attention to a related foundational principle: existence as inextricable interrelatedness, indifference to which brings disequilibrium. Interdependent diversity. Inextricable interrelatedness. These slogans speak truth to miasma, which undoubtedly accounts for their power and resonance, their appeal to a range of struggles across the world. When, as during this period, the battle is between forces invested in defying nature and those committed to defending life, it is the prophetic voices that galvanize and dynamize.

Aligned with nature
the wind at their back
the future belongs to them.

Spirit awaits their homecoming.

OUTOFTHEONE
MANY OUTOFTHEONE
INTHEONE MANY
E V E R Y INTHEONE
EVERY

OUT OF
THE ONE
MANY
IN
THE ONE
EVERY

Out of the One, Many. Typographical spread, 2021.
Design by Lata Mani and Bharath Haridas.

dark goddess

Dark Goddess who art everywhere
Hallowed is Thy name
Thy kingdom come, thy will be done
Here as in all the realms
Grant us today the intimacy we seek
And embrace us in all our tenderness
For you are fire and we are spark
Igniting the earth with longing

De Sidere 7

in silence the mind breathes
with nicolás grandi

HD, 2020, 1:02 MINUTES

"In Silence the Mind Breathes,"
Nicolás Grandi and Lata Mani, 2020.

https://doi.org/10.6084/m9.figshare.17018588

references

Ahluwahlia, Sanjam, Marie Agui Carter, Nicole Carr, et al. 2018. "In Scholarly Debates on #MeToo Survivor Support Should Take Precedence." Collective, May 23. https://medium.com/@nsscollectiveeditorial/collective-editorial-survivor-support-should-take-precedence-71a2f6230157.

Alcoff, Linda Martín. 2018. "This Is Not Just about Junot Díaz." *New York Times*, May 16. https://www.nytimes.com/2018/05/16/opinion/junot-diaz-metoo.html.

Alexander, Eban. 2012. *Proof of Heaven: A Neurosurgeon's Journey into the Afterlife*. New York: Simon and Schuster.

Alexander, Jacqui M. 2006. *Pedagogies of Crossing: Meditations on Feminism, Sexual Politics, Memory, and the Sacred*. Durham, NC: Duke University Press.

Almadhoun, Ghayath. 2017. *Adrenalin*. Translated by Catherine Cobham. Notre Dame, IN: Action Books.

Alter, Alexandra, Jonah Engel Bromwich, and Damien Cave. 2018. "The Writer Zinzi Clemmons Accuses Junot Díaz of Forcibly Kissing Her." *New York Times*, May 4. https://www.nytimes.com/2018/05/04/books/junot-diaz-accusations.html.

Anzaldúa, Gloria. 1987. *Borderlands/La Frontera: The New Mestiza*. San Francisco: Aunt Lute.

Appadurai, Arjun. 1996. *Modernity at Large: Cultural Dimensions of Globalization*. Minneapolis: University of Minnesota Press.

Bambara, Toni Cade. 1980. *The Salt Eaters.* New York: Random House.

Bambara, Toni Cade. [1981] 1983. Foreword. In *This Bridge Called My Back: Writings by Radical Women of Color*, edited by Cherríe Moraga and Gloria Anzaldúa, vi–viii. New York: Kitchen Table Women of Color Press.

Barad, Karen. 2007. *Meeting the Universe Halfway: The Entanglement of Matter and Meaning.* Durham, NC: Duke University Press.

Bombach, Alexandria, dir. 2018. *On Her Shoulders.* Trailer length: 2:35. Brooklyn, NY: Oscilloscope. https://www.youtube.com/watch?v=9RRE1DWK8cU.

Braidotti, Rosi. 2013. *The Posthuman.* Cambridge: Polity.

Braidotti, Rosi. 2019. *Posthuman Knowledge.* Cambridge: Polity.

Chakravarty, Dipesh. 2000. *Provincializing Europe: Postcolonial Thought and Historical Difference.* Princeton, NJ: Princeton University Press.

Chakravarty, Dipesh. 2018. *The Crises of Civilization: Exploring Global and Planetary Histories.* Oxford: Oxford University Press.

Chu, Andrea Long. 2018. "I Worked with Avital Ronell. I Believe Her Accuser." *Chronicle of Higher Education*, August 30. https://www.chronicle.com/article/I-Worked-With-Avital-Ronell-I/244415/.

de Jesús, Aisha Beliso, Cristina Beltrán, Laura Catelli, Elena Creef, Mabel Cuesta, Arlene Dávila, Zaire Dinzey, et al. 2018. "Open Letter against Media Treatment of Junot Díaz." *Chronicle of Higher Education*, May 14. https://www.chronicle.com/blogs/letters/open-letter-against-media-treatment-of-junot-diaz/.

de la Cadena, Marisol. 2015. *Earth Beings: Ecologies of Practice across Andean Worlds.* Durham, NC: Duke University Press.

Despret, Vinciane. 2016. *What Would Animals Say If We Asked the Right Questions?* Translated by Brett Buchanan. Minneapolis: University of Minnesota Press.

Díaz, Junot. 2018. "The Silence: The Legacy of Childhood Trauma." *New Yorker*, April 9. https://www.newyorker.com/magazine/2018/04/16/the-silence-the-legacy-of-childhood-trauma/.

Duggan, Lisa. 2018. "The Full Catastrophe." Bully Bloggers, August 18. https://bullybloggers.wordpress.com/2018/08/18/the-full-catastrophe/.

Eadie, Betty J. 1992. *Embraced by the Light.* New York: Bantam.

Escobar, Arturo. 2018. *Designs for the Pluriverse: Radical Interdependence, Autonomy, and the Making of Worlds.* Durham, NC: Duke University Press.

Flaherty, Colleen. 2018. "Junot Díaz, Feminism and Ethnicity." *Inside Higher Ed*, May 29. https://www.insidehighered.com/news/2018/05/29/rift-among-scholars-over-treatment-junot-d%C3%ADaz-he-faces-harassment-and-misconduct/.

Foucault, Michel. 1997. "The Masked Philosopher." In *Ethics, Subjectivity and Truth: The Essential Works of Michel Foucault 1954–1984*, vol. 1, ed. Paul Rabinow, 321–28. New York: New Press.

Frankenberg, Ruth, and Lata Mani, eds. 2013. *The Tantra Chronicles: Original Teachings from Devi, Shiva, Jesus, Mary, Moon* (self-pub.), epub. http://www.latamani.com/the-tantra-chronicles.

Gessen, Marsha. 2018. "An N.Y.U. Sexual-Harassment Case Has Spurred a Necessary Conversation About #MeToo." *New Yorker*, August 25. https://www.newyorker.com/news/our-columnists/an-nyu-sexual-harassment-case-has-spurred-a-necessary-conversation-about-metoo/.

Hall, Stuart. 1980. "Race, Articulation and Societies Structured in Dominance." In *Sociological Theories: Race and Colonialism*, 305–45. Paris: UNESCO.

Hall, Stuart. 1996. "The Problem of Ideology: Marxism without Guarantees." In *Stuart Hall: Critical Dialogues in Cultural Studies*, ed. David Morley and Kuan-Hsing Chen, 24–45. London: Routledge.

Hall, Stuart. 2019. *Essential Essays*. Vol. 1, *Foundations of Cultural Studies*, edited by David Morley. Durham, NC: Duke University Press.

Hall, Stuart. 2019. *Essential Essays*. Vol. 2, *Identity and Diaspora*, edited by David Morley. Durham, NC: Duke University Press.

Haraway, Donna. 1988. "Situated Knowledges: The Science Question and the Privilege of Partial Perspective." *Feminist Studies* 14, no. 3: 575–99.

Haraway, Donna. 1991. *Simians, Cyborgs, and Women: The Reinvention of Nature*. London: Free Association Books.

Haraway, Donna. 2003. *The Companion Species Manifesto: Dogs, People, and Significant Otherness*. Chicago: Prickly Paradigm.

Haraway, Donna. 2008. *When Species Meet*. Minneapolis: University of Minnesota Press.

Haraway, Donna. 2016. *Staying with the Trouble: Making Kin in the Chthulucene*. Durham, NC: Duke University Press.

Krishnan, Kavita. 2017. "'It's Like Blackening Faces': Why I Am Uneasy with the Name and Shame List of Sexual Harassers." Scroll.in, October 25. https://scroll.in/article/855399/its-like-blackening-faces-why-i-am-uneasy-with-the-name-and-shame-list-of-sexual-harassers.

Latour, Bruno. 2017. *Facing Gaia: Eight Lectures on the New Climatic Regime*. Cambridge: Polity.

Latour, Bruno. 2018. *Down to Earth: Politics in the New Climatic Regime*. Cambridge: Polity.

Leiter, Brian. 2018. "Blaming the Victim Is Apparently OK When the Accused in a Title IX Proceeding Is a Feminist Literary Theorist." *Leiter Reports: A Philosophy Blog*, June 10. https://leiterreports.typepad.com/blog/2018

/06/blaming-the-victim-is-apparently-ok-when-the-accused-is-a-feminist
-literary-theorist.html/.

Mandelbrot, Benoît. 1982. *The Fractal Geometry of Nature*. New York: W. H. Freeman.

Mani, Lata. 2009. *SacredSecular: Contemplative Cultural Critique*. Abingdon, UK: Routledge.

Mani, Lata. 2011. *Interleaves: Ruminations on Illness and Spiritual Life*. New Delhi: Yoda Press. Originally self-published in 2001.

Mani, Lata. 2013. *The Integral Nature of Things: Critical Reflections on the Present*. Abingdon, UK: Routledge.

Mani, Lata. 2014. "Sex and the Signal-Free Corridor: Towards a New Feminist Imaginary." *Economic and Political Weekly* 49, no. 6 (February 8): 26–29.

Mani, Lata. 2015. "Writing the Present." *Economic and Political Weekly* 50, no. 49 (December 5): 24–27.

Mbembe, Achille. 2020. "The Universal Right to Breathe." Translated by Carolyn Shread. *In the Moment* blog, *Critical Inquiry*, April 13. https://critinq.wordpress.com/2020/04/13/the-universal-right-to-breathe/.

Menon, Nivedita. 2017. "Statement by Feminists on Facebook Campaign to 'Name and Shame.'" *Kafila*, October 24. https://kafila.online/2017/10/24/statement-by-feminists-on-facebook-campaign-to-name-and-shame/.

Minh-ha, Trinh T. 1989. *Woman Native Other*. Bloomington: Indiana University Press.

Mohanty, Chandra Talpade. 1987. "Feminist Encounters: Locating the Politics of Experience." *Copyright* 1, no. 1: 30–44.

Moraga, Cherríe L. 2011. *A Xicana Codex of Changing Consciousness: Writings, 2000–2010*. Durham, NC: Duke University Press.

Moraga, Cherríe, and Gloria Anzaldúa, eds. 1981. *This Bridge Called My Back: Writings by Radical Women of Color*. Watertown, MA: Persephone.

Morley, David, and Kuan-Hsing Chen, eds. 1996. *Stuart Hall: Critical Dialogues in Cultural Studies*. London: Routledge.

Mukwege, Denis. 2016. "Denis Mukwege: The Man Who Mends Women." Video clip from *The 51 Percent*, posted by France 24, February 19. YouTube video, 11:18. https://www.youtube.com/watch?v=PmCE9eUeqDI&t=2s.

Nhat Hahn, Thich. 1999. "Interrelationship." In *Call Me by My True Names: The Collected Poems of Thich Nhat Hahn*, 154. Berkeley: Parallax Press.

Online Desk. 2017. "Important to Name Perpetrators, Says V Geetha on Raya Sarkar's Crowd-Sourced List of Sexual Harassers." *New Indian Express*, October 27. http://www.newindianexpress.com/nation/2017/oct/27/important-to-name-perpetrators-says-v-geetha-on-raya-sarkars-crowd-sourced-list-of-sexual-harasser-1684340.html/.

Orwell, George. 1949. *1984*. London: Secker and Warburg.

Parker, Pat. 1978. "For the White Person Who Wants to Know How to Be My Friend." From *Movement in Black*. https://condor.depaul.edu/mwilson /multicult/patparker.htm.

Perry, Imani. 2019. *Breathe: A Letter to My Sons*. Boston: Beacon.

Povinelli, Elizabeth. 2016. *Geontologies: A Requiem to Late Liberalism*. Durham, NC: Duke University Press.

Rich, Adrienne. 1986. "Notes Toward a Politics of Location (1984)." In *Blood, Bread, and Poetry*. New York: Norton, 210–31.

Robin, Corey. 2018. "The Unsexy Truth about the Avital Ronell Scandal." *Chronicle of Higher Education*, August 20. https://www.chronicle.com /article/The-Unsexy-Truth-About-the/244314/.

Robinson, Amy Elizabeth. 2018. "On Power and Aporia in the Academy: A Response in Three Parts." Medium, August 19. https://medium.com/@ amyelizabethrobinson/on-power-and-aporia-in-the-academy-a-response -in-three-parts-f7387c346ffa.

Rodriguez, Alicita. 2017. "How to Know You Are a Woman in a Junot Diaz Novel." *Copper Nickel*, no. 24 (Spring): 80.

Rowena, Jenny. 2017. "The 'Sexual Harassment' Discourse: A Bahujan Woman's Perspective." *RAIOT*, November 21. http://raiot.in/the-sexual-harassment -discourse-a-bahujan-womans-perspective/.

Said, Edward. 1979. *Orientalism*. New York: Vintage.

Sainath, Palagummi. 2016. "P Sainath Speaks at #StandWithJNU." Lecture at Jawaharlal Nehru University, February 19. YouTube video, 1:00:26. https://www.youtube.com/watch?v=k3dq6pApmhk.

Sandoval, Chela. 1991. "U.S. Third World Feminism: The Theory and Method of Oppositional Consciousness in the Postmodern World." *Genders: Journal of Social Theory, Representation, Race, Gender, Sex*, no. 10: 1–24.

Shankar, Karthik. 2017. "Why I Published a List of Sexual Predators in Academia." *BuzzFeed News*, October 25. https://www.buzzfeed.com /karthikshankar/why-i-published-a-list-of-sexual-predators-in-academia.

Shreerekha. 2018. "In the Wake of His Damage." Rumpus, May 12. https:// therumpus.net/2018/05/in-the-wake-of-his-damage/.

Slater, Joanna. 2019. "Why Protests Are Erupting over India's New Citizenship Law." *Washington Post*, December 19. https://www.washingtonpost.com /world/asia_pacific/why-indias-citizenship-law-is-so-contentious/2019/12 /17/35d75996-2042-11ea-b034-de7dc2b5199b_story.html.

Stengers, Isabelle. 2010. *Cosmopolitics I*. Minneapolis: University of Minnesota Press.

Stengers, Isabelle. 2011. *Cosmopolitics II*. Minneapolis: University of Minnesota Press.

Sunitha, A., Uma Bhrugubanda, Vasudha Nagaraj, and Lakshmi Kutty. 2017. "The 'List' and the Task of Rearranging Academic Relationships." *Engage* 52, no. 47 (November 24). https://www.epw.in/engage/article/list-and -task-rearranging-academic-relationships.

Tiwary, Ishita, and Tarangini Sriraman. 2017. "How Young Women in Indian Academia Feel about the List." *BuzzFeed News*, November 22. https:// www.buzzfeed.com/ishitatiwary/how-young-women-in-indian-academia -feel-about-the-list.

Tsing, Anna Lowenhaupt. 2015. *The Mushroom at the End of the World: On the Possibility of Life in Capitalist Ruins.* Princeton, NJ: Princeton University Press.

Vemula, Rohith. 2016. "Full Text: Dalit Scholar Rohith Vemula's Suicide Note." *Times of India*, January 19. http://timesofindia.indiatimes.com /city/hyderabad/Full-text-Dalit-scholar-Rohith-Vemulas-suicide-note /articleshowprint/50634646.cms.